CALLED TO THE BAR

An account of the first 21 years of the Campaign for Real Ale

Published by the Campaign for Real Ale 1992

© CAMRA Ltd. 1992

Registered Office:
34 Alma Road, St Albans, Hertfordshire AL1 3BW

Edited by Roger Protz and Tony Millns

Cover illustration by Bill Tidy

Typeset and printed by Linneys, Newgate Lane, Mansfield,
Nottinghamshire NG18 2PA

The Editors acknowledge the generous assistance of many CAMRA members in preparing this book, especially Andrew Sangster of CAMRA HQ for research help and Ella Pritchard for preparing clean typescript of contributors' copy.

ISBN 1 85249 065 9

CALLED TO THE BAR

An account of the first 21 years of the Campaign for Real Ale

Edited by Roger Protz and Tony Millns

Published by the Campaign for Real Ale

f. real ale, a name sometimes applied to draught beer that has been brewed and stored in the traditional way, and which has undergone secondary fermentation of the yeast in the container from which it is dispensed; also called 'cask-conditioned' beer;

1972 *What's Brewing* Oct., Mr A– B–..is ripping out the keg taps and replacing them with real ale from wooden barrels. 1973, C. Hᴜᴛᴛ *Death of Eng. Pub* i. 25 The beer-drinker who feels strongly about the declining quality of his pint has two organisations he can turn to..–the long-established Society for the Preservation of Beers from the Wood, and the more recently formed, more militant CAMRA (Campaign for Real Ale). 1974 *Good Beer Guide* (CAMRA). *:* The real ale we are talking about has to stand up to three tests: in the way it is brewed, the way it is stored and the way it is served. 1976 *Evening Standard* 29 Dec., The most popular of about a dozen real ales brought in from distant parts to a growing number of pubs in the capital. 1980 *Times* 23 December 8/3 In the 1970s..the 'real ale' fashion took hold.

This definition, which appears in the Second Edition (1991) of the *Oxford English Dictionary*, was the subject of correspondence between Dr Robert Burchfield, the OED Editor-in-Chief, and Tony Millns, then CAMRA Chairman, in 1983.

CONTENTS

Foreword

Setting the Scene:

Turning Points:

Personal Views:

CONTENTS (continued)

FOREWORD

Since it was founded in 1971, over 100,000 people have at one time or another been members of CAMRA.

But even that figure is a small proportion of the number of people who, by millions of individual acts of choice, ordered one beer rather than another across the bars of pubs and clubs the length and breadth of the country.

CAMRA created the climate for and awareness of the possibility of choice, and helped to hold out the promise that choice might be fulfilled. But no brewer would have responded – or, in the case of those few who stayed true to traditional cask-conditioned beer, been able to survive for long – if there had not been evidence of continued and increasing public demand.

That demand was stimulated and publicised by CAMRA in its early stages of existence as a single-issue campaign dedicated to preserving real ale. In this simple aim, it has surely been more successful than most early members would have dared dream.

But it has gone on from that success to broaden its scope. Having won the first battle, beer drinkers have realised that, to paraphrase John Curran's remark, the price of liberty of choice is eternal vigilance. That vigilance needs to be maintained not merely locally, nor even nationally, but internationally: for beer is now a product in a truly common market.

Within that international market, CAMRA will always have as its first concern the promotion of a wider appreciation of those unique and flavourful cask-conditioned British ales which it saved from extinction.

This book tells that story, in the words of many of the people who were most closely involved. But all of those 100,000 members and former members of CAMRA could tell other parts of it, or tell it differently but no less validly. And without the millions of people who agreed, and exercised their choice to demand good beer on every possible opportunity, none of the success would ever have happened. It is to them – the beer drinkers of Britain – that we dedicate this book.

Roger Protz and Tony Millns

THE BRITISH BREWING INDUSTRY SINCE 1750

Background

IT IS MUCH easier to stress the importance of the brewing industry in 1750 than it is to present a sharply focused account of its organisation. Beer was a basic necessity of life. Gregory King reckoned in 1695 that no less than twenty-eight per cent of annual per capita expenditure went on ale and beer; the Prince Regent stoutly maintained, 'Beer and beef has made us what we are'. Certainly, demand for the national drink was vast, inelastic and universal. If it was consumed by everyone in varying strengths and in increasing amounts in the eighteenth century, its production nevertheless poses a problem for historians since it fell into three broad and ill-defined categories with wide regional variations.

First, there were many gentlemen, all farmers employing much labour, and institutions like colleges, hospitals and poor houses who brewed their own beer. Even the poor struggled to produce a barrel at harvest-time, and Cobbett in his *Cottage Economy* (1822) devoted almost a quarter of its contents to 'brewing beer'. As much as half of all output was privately brewed in 1700; one and a half centuries later it was still reckoned to be a fifth. Secondly, the majority of inns and ale houses produced their own beer in 1750. According to the excise statistics there were no fewer than 48,421 victuallers producing 2,227,200 barrels of strong beer and 1,139,400 of small or table beer, although by 1799 their numbers had been reduced by more than a half. In these public houses, or at least in their outbuildings, the landlord and his servants mashed a few bushels of malt every ten or fourteen days. Usually they brewed no more than was consumed on their premises and by their private trade, although it is evident that during the second half of the eighteenth century, especially after the 1790s when duties on malt, beer, and hops rose sharply, they relied increasingly upon beer supplied by common brewers. In fact there was a sharp regional divide: publican brewers were especially numerous in the Midlands, the South-West, Wales and the North, whereas in Surrey, Middlesex, Berkshire, Hertfordshire, Oxfordshire, Hampshire, Sussex and Kent there were virtually no publicans who brewed their own beer. For example, in Yorkshire two-thirds of all beer was brewed by victuallers as late as 1825, whereas two years later in East Anglia and the Home Counties only 820 of 9984 victuallers were still brewing. Unfortunately, as Peter Clark discovered when the wrote *The English Alehouse* (1983), very little documentation – if it ever existed – has survived concerning this significant branch of beer production.

Thirdly, there were the common brewers. For centuries in London, with its great concentration of population, brewing had fallen into the hands of common brewers. Already in 1700 there were almost 200, brewing an average 5,000 barrels each. A century later the five biggest London breweries produced over a 100,000 apiece. Indeed, some of the largest of all eighteenth-century industrial enterprises were London porter breweries. Peter Mathias traced their evolution in splendid detail thirty years ago: no area of the industry has been better surveyed. With a larger consumer demand in the capital, and serving an extensive 'country' trade accessible by water carriage, these breweries benefited from economies of scale which were derived from handling huge quantities of porter, a cheapish, strong and high-coloured mass-produced beer. All the notable innovations in making beer output more reliable were introduced first in these great breweries – thermometers, hydrometers and attemperators. And in the 1780s and 1790s they were prominent in their adoption of the latest steam engines. They also went a step further in the organisation of their enterprises when they began to 'tie' their retail outlets, by either acquiring outright ownership or, more frequently, by making loans for the expensive London leases of those publicans who took their beer.

London took the lead in all these developments, but in towns everywhere which grew rapidly with the population explosions of the late eighteenth-century similar, less spectacular, transformations in the scale of brewing took place. The extent of these changes appears to have been dependent upon two factors. First, the size of breweries around 1800 was limited by carriage restrictions since beer, of great bulk and low value, was uneconomical to transport any distance along even the best roads of Georgian England. Therefore, any appreciable changes in the scale of provincial brewing relied upon the concentration of demand which only a large, urban market provided. Secondly, as we have already noted, there were very marked geographical differences in the spread of common brewers, between roughly the East and South on the one hand and the Midlands, Wales and some northern counties on the other. These differences seem to be best explained by reference to the barley and malt trade.

All good malting barley was grown in the dry eastern and south-eastern counties, and those brewers that produced malt as well as beer derived benefits from this duality of business which allowed their breweries to expand. Already by 1800, there were towns in East Anglia, like Colchester, Ipswich, Great Yarmouth, Norwich and King's Lynn, where common brewers were doing a trade of several thousands of barrels annually, owning their own maltings and many public houses. As early as 1800 Patteson's Norwich brewery produced 20,000 barrels, and thirty years later when it had amalgamated with Steward's the firm owned or leased 198 public houses. It was probably rather exceptional but there are other examples, Cobb in Margate, Best in Chatham and Brakspear in Henley to name but three, where similar developments were taking place after the 1790s. Even in strongholds of victualler brewing, like Leeds, Hull and Manchester, the common brewer was in the ascendant. The movement appears to have been speeded up by the sharp increases in duties and prices during the French Wars (1793-1815) and also by the demand for more consistent beers which the common brewer achieved more readily with his application of the new technology. Different regional tastes were not eliminated. Robert Brakspear, the Henley brewer, reckoned 'that a weak stomach will as soon digest pork [or] pease soup as Burton, Yorkshire and Nottingham ales. They make excellent bird-lime and

Table 1
United Kingdom beer output, consumption and real wages, 1830-1914
(annual averages)

Years	Beer output (million standard barrels)	Consumption per head (gallons)	Average real wages (1850=100)
1830-34	14.8	21.6	–
1835-39	16.4	22.6	–
1840-44	14.8	19.5	–
1845-49	15.2	19.4	–
1850-54	16.4	21.1	101.2
1855-59	17.7	22.0	96.2
1860-64	20.4	24.6	105.8
1865-69	24.8	28.8	111.6
1870-74	28.1	31.1	127.4
1875-79	31.4	33.2	132.0
1880-84	28.2	29.1	137.2
1885-89	29.3	28.4	149.4
1890-94	32.1	29.8	164.0
1895-99	35.2	31.2	176.4
1900-04	35.9	30.2	175.2
1905-09	33.8	27.3	173.0
1910-14	34.7	27.0	171.2

Source: B R Mitchell and P Deane, *Abstract of British Historical Statistics* (1962), pp. 343-5 and G B Wilson, *Alcohol and the Nation* (1940), pp. 333-5, 369-70.

when simmered over a gentle fire, make the most excellent sticking plaster for old strains'. But the differences between the sound beers of common brewers with good keeping qualities and the variable concoctions of victuallers and home brewers grew. By 1830 the former were increasingly deriving a competitive edge in terms of cost, profitability and quality from the growing sale of their output and they began to tie their retail outlets by ownership, lease or loan.

Therefore when the Wellington government in 1830, nervous of uprising, anxious to suppress a buoyant spirits trade and eager to reduce living costs, decided to free the trade in beer in the summer of 1830 it attempted to balance the interests of brewers against its aim to reduce the price of beer. The legislation has a 1980s ring in its intention to undermine vested interests and induce competition. The Act therefore did two things: it bought off the brewers by abolishing the beer duty of ten shillings a barrel (that on malt was retained until 1880); it created a new type of public house, which was intended to reverse the growing tendency of common brewers, at least in London and the South-East, to control the retail outlets of beer. Any householder who paid rates and could afford the two guineas excise licence was allowed to sell beer on his own premises. Within six months almost 25,000 new beer-house keepers had paid the excise fee, a number which rose to 45,417 in 1838. Outlets to sell beer (not spirits) were almost doubled in less than a decade. In the long run, however, the Act created a paradise for common brewers. They were able to reduce the price of beer appreciably and supply most of these new outlets, for the large majority did not brew their own beer at least after the 1850s.

If the Beer Act provided an opportunity to stimulate consumption and a lax licensing context between 1830 and 1870, it does not entirely explain why the urban classes of Victorian Britain turned increasingly to drink. The evidence supplied in Table 1 is quite extraordinary but this is not the place to supply an extended explanation of it. Most members of the employed urban working classes were better off, with more money after the mid 1840s to spend on food, drink and leisure, and those middle-class values which preached the virtues of abstinence and control in matters of sex, alcohol and violence were never all-pervasive, especially before the 1870s. In the first flush of its modest liberation the working classes of the early Victorian city turned in its celebration to beer, providing brewers with golden opportunities. Of course, temperance took a strong hold in a society where alcohol consumption rose so sharply in the half-century after 1830, but this was more than compensated for by rising consumption and the fact that private and publican brewing contracted from as much as two-thirds of output in 1830 to a mere one per cent in 1914. Their production grew, possibly by as much as eight times, between the Beer Act and the First World War. Within a market growth of these dimensions, and protected by a tied retailing umbrella after the 1880s, it was no wonder that some of the greatest fortunes and business successes of the Victorian period were created.

The Rise of Burton

In London where growth was achieved upon the most solid foundations, in 1831, 115 common brewers produced a total output of 2,213,750 standard barrels (36 gallons of 1055° gravity); in 1880, 113 – the number of brewers had fallen to as low as sixty-four in 1851 – produced 5,003,300 standard barrels. But as early as 1830 the twelve leading firms concentrated as much as eighty-five per cent of the production of strong beer in their great porter breweries, and half a century later ten firms accounted for around seventy-two per cent of output. Even in the oligopolistic London market there were newcomers throughout the period, but the question that interests the historian of brewing in London in these years is how the great porter brewers of 1830 adapted to change and competition.

The problem is not easy to unravel because we know little in detail about the history of any of the big London breweries in this half-century. Peter Mathias showed how, in the century after 1730, the dozen or so largest firms emerged, supplying the rapidly growing population of the capital and its immediate environs with its preferred drink – porter, which was cheap, distinctive, matured, although easy to adulterate. In terms of investment and technology, and of the scale and complexity of their enterprise, these firms came to dominate London's drink trade. In 1830, had that creature of the

1980s trade the brewing analyst been invented, he would have looked no further than London for his market leaders; fifty years later he would have needed to discuss developments in Burton-on-Trent, Dublin and other centres like Bristol and Edinburgh, or even Alton and Tadcaster. Quite simply London lost its lead in the mid-nineteenth century.

Explanations probably need to concentrate around two foci. First, the passion for porter diminished: slowly to the 1850s, very rapidly after the 1870s. Shifts in changes in taste 130 to 150 years ago are now difficult to pinpoint with accuracy, but the evidence suggests that mild and then pale ales made increasing inroads into the traditional porter market. Secondly, the great porter brewers, principally Barclay Perkins, Whitbread and Reid, were rather slow to adapt to these changing tastes. Their breweries needed substantial reconstruction to produce ale, and soft water from London wells did not produce good, bright Burton-style ales until they began to be treated with gypsum after 1870. But the real explanation is more likely to rest in the conservatism of their management. The great London brewing partnerships do not seem to have changed much in this period. In comparison with Burton ale brewers, who made the pace in brewing developments after 1840, they were slow to introduce the new brewing science which emerged from the 1860s, they were slow to appoint accountants, and they were slow to adopt trade marks and advertising. Locked into their world of traditional production and the loan-tie arrangement (whereby brewers made substantial capital loans to publicans in return for exclusive rights of supply) peculiar to the 6,000 or so London public houses, they were content to return five per cent on their large capitals. Good management consisted of carefully manipulating marginal costs on materials and overheads to maximise profits, and astutely judging the size of their loans to public houses. Only one of the great porter breweries (Trumans) managed to double output in this half-century, whereas a number of newly-founded ale brewers – Charringtons, Mann, Crossman & Paulin and Courage – besides well-established concerns like Watneys and Combes achieved extraordinary growth in these years. After 1860 the Burton brewers and later other regional brewers were, through the agency system, able to invade the London market to make it highly competitive by the 1880s.

In contrast with the measured progress of the great London brewers between 1830 and 1880, the most rapid advances in the British brewing industry were made in Burton-on-Trent. It is a curious story well-known to economic historians of the nineteenth century. Brewing in the town had a long history, and by 1800 it was renowned for its export of fine pale ales principally to the Baltic. When this trade collapsed with the Napoleonic Blockade, the handful of small breweries in Burton were forced to shift rapidly into the London and Indian export trades. In both markets its 'Indian' Pale Ales (IPA) met with success, but so long as transport relied upon long and expensive canal connections with London they remained severely limited. On the eve of the completion of its national rail connection in 1839, Burton boasted nine breweries with a total output of between 60,000 and 70,000 barrels a year. The basis of Burton's success was its extremely hard water, containing magnesium and calcium sulphate deposits and requiring high applications of hops. The resulting beer was a bright, strong, distinctive ale, which looked good – unlike the somewhat murky porter – in the new glassware which was everywhere replacing the old pewter drinking vessels. Burton ales became increasingly the accepted drink of the Victorian middle and skilled artisan classes. Of course, these would have made no progress without the railways which allowed 36 gallon barrels to be transported quickly anywhere in Britian for around three shillings each (about five per cent of wholesale prices). Success was instant. Burton's output trebled every ten years between 1850 and 1880 from around 300,000 to three million barrels. In this great growth two firms stood paramount, Bass and Allsopp. By the late 1870s Bass produced close on a million barrels; Allsopp at its peak, in 1876, 918,000. They rapidly became household names; their owners were thrust into the highly select coterie of Victorian millionaires. Not only were they leaders in terms of scale, but in their management styles and above all in the way that they utilised and encouraged scientific research in brewing. They were able to produce vast quantities of a high quality product which did not need storing for several months like porter, or even years in the case of old ales, that the London and provincial brewers prided themselves upon. In the control of their own maltings, often scattered across eastern England (Bass had thirty-seven in the mid-1880s), in their achievement of rapid growth by the use of discounts, trade-marks and agency marketing they were pace setters. Selling a quarter of their output in London, everywhere penetrating the free trade, their success was trumpeted across Britain.

In this atmosphere it was inevitable that Bass and Allsopp would have their imitators, eager to take advantage of the water, the Burton method of producing quick maturing beers, and the agency and rail system of retailing. By the mid-1880s there were thirty-one breweries in the town, producing three million barrels a year with a work-force of 8,000. Not all were successful: the Burton Brewery Company had a chequered history, and there was a fair turnover of smaller firms. Yet Burton firms like T F Salt and Worthingtons did well, and others who joined them in the second rank were ale-producing subsidiaries of celebrated London brewers – Ind Coope from Romford (who commenced their Burton operations in 1856), Charringtons (1872), Trumans (1873) and Mann, Crossman & Paulin (1875). Hugh Charrington put the reasons for these moves succinctly in 1883: 'We could not brew a glass of beer equal to the Burton brewers and we were compelled to come down here to brew beer as the people would have it'. In fact, when the industry became increasingly competitive after 1880, the way forward in Burton was much less easy, but in the preceding forty years its story was one of extraordinary success and dynamism.

It is much easier to make generalisations about brewing in London and Burton during the free trade era than it is elsewhere in Britain. There are two problems: numbers and lack of documentation. First, setting aside publican brewers which contracted so sharply across the nineteenth century, there were still 2,649 commercial or common brewers in 1880, a figure little lower than that of forty years earlier. It is a large number of firms for the business historian to handle. Secondly, although there was a large number of Victorian country brewers because some documentation survived the process of post-1885 amalgamation, very seldom has a large enough archive survived a century of sorting, salvage drives, and removal to allow a thorough going reconstruction of a firm's decision-making and action.

Because so many country breweries survived to 1880, and they prospered in all shapes and sizes, it is difficult to pinpoint the typical country brewery. It is obvious that until the 1870s, although the entry to the industry was by inheritance rather than purchase, there were apparently large numbers of newcomers, at least amongst the smaller producers, and progress could still be made by an enterprising entrant in the free trade. But the point about numbers and newcomers hides the essential fact about Victorian country breweries. There were some regional breweries – and the list is very long – like Vaux, Mitchell & Butler, Peter Walker, Threlfalls, John Smith, Tetley, Newcastle, Boddingtons, Georges, Simonds, Brain, McEwan and Younger – who made, in their own way, as rapid progress as the market leaders in Burton and London. By 1880 there were no fewer than 203, mostly provincial brewers, who brewed between 20,000 and 100,000 barrels annually, and twenty-three between 100,000 and 500,000 barrels. Within these bands were all the successful commercial brewers who had thrived in the mid-Victorian period.

How were they able to achieve their advance from concerns in the 1830s, brewing 10,000 to 20,000 barrels a year, to establishments turning out 100,000 and, exceptionally, 200,000 plus barrels half a century later? The demand side of the explanation is familiar: a rapidly rising urban population with increasing living standards and a predilection to spend any surplus on beer. In terms of supply, transport improvements, which freed the brewers from their traditional constraint of a highly local market, and the attrition of publican brewers were important. It is clear that after 1830 the publican and private brewers were under real pressure from commercial brewers. Partly this was a question of taxation. With the sole tax now falling upon malt, extraction rates were all significant. The publican brewer was not able to match the commercial brewers in this respect and maintain a quality product; he could not produce the range of beers all Victorian common brewers endeavoured to produce – pale, mild and strong ales, porter and stout; he simply did not have the turnover to achieve a regular supply of fresh pale and mild ales which were in such vogue after 1850. Yet in some areas, like the West Midlands and Yorkshire, even until the early 1890s, many publican brewers survived. Nevertheless, nationally numbers more than halved from 1840 to 1880, before they nosedived in the period to 1914.

In the boom conditions of the mid-Victorian drink trade the commercial brewer thrived. There were no general rules of advance, no accepted way forward. Some clearly did well because they were well placed in major cities and were by 1830 generating healthy profits like Georges in Bristol and Steward & Patteson in Norwich. And there were in Tadcaster, Alton and Wrexham – towns which became mini-Burtons – brewers who were able to brew excellent ales from ample supplies of hard water and distribute them over wide areas via the agency system. Clearly, some brewers relied largely upon urban markets on their doorstep and neighbouring country trades;

others managed to push their beers more extensively on the Burton model of distribution. Those who made most progress tended to brew passable imitations of Burton ales, built or reconstructed their breweries on up-to-date models, especially in the late 1860s and early 1870s when profitability was at its height, and kept abreast of the latest technical aids, if not science as such. Some relied heavily on the tied-house system like Steward & Patteson in Norwich; others, like Simonds of Reading, ran a 'mixed' system, owning around seventy houses in 1870 but achieving an annual barrelage of over 100,000 by 1880, largely by their exertions in supplying railway and army refreshment outlets. Then there was the Tetley 'model', whereby the partnership grew into one of the most successful of all regional breweries, producing an output of around 200,000 barrels by the early 1890s without any tied estate. Smaller breweries like Elgood, Webster and Brakspear made modest progress largely through their own stock of public houses, adding one or two perhaps every other year as profits and availability allowed. Greene King made headway in rural East Anglia almost entirely in the free trade before 1868; then suddenly, the presence of a new and thrusting rival drove them both into headlong acquisition almost twenty years before the race to acquire public houses became ubiquitous.

Obviously some brewers were more enterprising than others, some relied largely on a tied estate, others achieved considerable growth without this umbrella. Almost all malted barley on their own account, many generated a level of profits which made investment regular. After 1830 market conditions were right for the commercial brewer to prosper. All the evidence about the disposition of their growing wealth and their activity in political and country life underlines this fact.

The Tie

During the thirty years before the outbreak of the First World War the brewing industry changed quite rapidly. As so often in these matters, the catalyst was a relative stagnation in demand. Its severity must not be exaggerated: the mid-and late-1890s were years of exceptional prosperity for brewers, but per capita consumption never again reached the height of the late 1870s and everywhere after 1900 brewers were complaining of drinkers turning away from the public house, the old citadel of working-class leisure. Certainly after 1900 real wages declined (see Table 1), and there was a demonstrable preference for consumers to buy cheap ready-made clothing and shoes, machine-produced furniture and packaged foodstuffs in place of drink. Leisure outlets, the music-hall, football and cheap railway excursions enjoyed enormous popularity. These shifts in consumer demand were as significant in their impact on the drink trade as Temperance and Nonconformist attacks which were at their height in these years.

Changes in consumption patterns, although extremely important in trimming brewers' profits after 1900, were only one aspect inducing change. There were three others of significance which were in part interrelated – the restriction of licences, the popularity of limited liability after 1886, and the subsequent stampede to tie houses. A discussion of this last point returns us to the question of declining profitability and consumption after 1900.

As with the stagnation in consumption after 1880, it is easy to exaggerate the impact of licensing restriction after 1870. What happened was that the tide turned, and the industry had to work in an increasingly hostile environment to 1914 and beyond. Undoubtedly the restriction, after half a century of expansion, was real enough, and it was a prime cause in driving brewers after 1880 into acquiring the freehold of almost all those public houses that were either 'free', leased, or, in London, controlled by loan-tie arrangements. The figures for the number of licences in England and Wales are set out in Table 2:

Table 2
Total of on-licences, England & Wales, 1831-1915

Year	Total of on-licences	Population ('000s)	Population per public house
1831 a	82,466	13,994	170
1841	89,622	15,929	178
1855	102,307	18,829	184
1875	109,346	24,045	220
1886	103,593	27,522	266
1896	101,903	30,803	302
1906	98,894	34,342	347
1915	86,626	35,284 b	407

Source: G B Wilson, *Alcohol and the Nation* (1940), pp. 380, 394-5; B R Mitchell and P Deane, *Abstract of British Historical Statistics* (1962), pp. 8-10.

Notes: a The 1831 and 1841 figures are not strictly comparable with the later ones quoted in Wilson, p. 380. They are of retailers and publicans with beer and cider licences plus 'on' licensed beer houses.

b Civilians only.

The crucial legislation which underpins the contraction of licences was that enacted by Gladstone between 1869 and 1874, but its application depended upon the licensing magistrates. The majority, especially the rural squirearchy and Anglican clergy who formed most of their numbers, were by no means motivated by the Temperance – Nonconformist animus against the drink trade. But the legislation of 1869 to 1874, the constant wave of temperance publicity and legislative attempts to secure at least Local Options, and a series of High Court judgements (especially the celebrated *Sharpe v Wakefield*, 1891), meant that licensing magistrates were vigilant because they were ever exposed to attack. Even Conservative governments, traditionally friendly to brewing interests, could not resist renewed attempts to restrict further the number of licences. Their Royal Commission on the subject, reporting in 1899, favoured this course of action. In fact brewers were not totally opposed to restriction. In some city centres the need for the curtailment of licences was evident even to the most rabid Tory brewer. But all demanded proper compensation for the large losses the removal of a licence entailed.

Eventually, after much discussion and a real move by magistrates in 1902 to 1903 to refuse licences, a major Act was passed in 1904 which set out a proper scheme of compensation. Although the fund was provided by a levy raised on the brewers themselves, the Act was represented as a 'Brewers' Endowment Act'. Certainly most brewers, as their records reveal, worked out very carefully the off-loading of some of their less economic houses. The Liberal government after 1906, hurried along by Lloyd George in this respect, had the strongest anti-drink bias, although few of its leading Cabinet members appear to have practised in private what they preached in public. In 1909 to 1910 its attack on the tied-house system was at the heart of its constitutional collision with the House of Lords. In its implications for the brewers the controversy centered upon the Government's proposals 'to hound the trade out of existence' by increasing steeply the duty on public houses. In the event the old revenue of some £1.9 million was merely doubled (a levy of £5 million had been gloomily forecast by the industry), and brewers everywhere contested the rateable valuation of their public houses on the grounds that their value was diminished by a duty which now equalled half the annual rental. Board meeting minutes after 1900 commonly reveal the agonies of brewers in their discussions of these issues and how they began to formulate policies which would see them through the adverse conditions. So long as the number of public houses grew and beer consumption increased there appeared little incentive for brewers to tie public houses in their area by direct purchase. True, some breweries in the country had expanded by the slow but regular acquisition of houses since the early nineteenth century, but the larger Burton breweries, Guinness, and a considerable number of breweries in the Midlands and North had achieved even better rates of growth in the free trade. London breweries, manipulating a hybrid structure of control by the loan-tie, occupied in effect a half-way stage between the polarities of the Burton agency system and those breweries in the South-East and Liverpool which owned large numbers of houses by the 1870s. After 1880, when licence restriction and falling consumption (output fell by as much as sixteen per cent between 1876 and 1881) began to bite, breweries looked to the defence of their trade. The way ahead in an increasingly hostile environment, after half a century of continuous expansion, was by forward integration. Almost every free house, or those partially controlled through lease or loan-tie, was acquired by direct purchase before 1914, when it is reckoned that ninety per cent of all the licensed property in Britian had been bought by the brewers. The question for historians of the industry is to examine how breweries raised the necessary finance and what the consequences were for the industry.

The issue is made more complex because not all breweries started in the race to acquire public houses around 1880 with an equal handicap. Some breweries, like Allsopp and Tetley, owned no houses before the late 1880s as a matter of policy, and few London brewers had acquired long leases on their pubs before the mid-1880s. On the other hand many country breweries had secured more sizeable estates by 1880. Possibly some forty per cent of all licensed properties were controlled by 1870. Sale notices of breweries in the press seem to confirm this, although regional differences must always be stressed. These breweries continued to grow, often forced into an accelerated pace after 1880, largely by ploughing profits into buying further tied property. But every brewery, whatever its size, was pushed along by the heady pace of acquisition. None – besides Guinness which retailed a special product – that wished to survive could fail to enter the race. Indeed, when the market for houses began to dry up and prices advanced very sharply after 1895, the only way forward for the larger brewers was to swallow up their smaller rivals. The period 1880 to 1914 saw the beginning of a century of amalgamation and merger amongst brewers: the number of common brewers fell by forty-four per cent in these years whilst their average output increased by 130 per cent. Of course, the pace of acquisition, both of public houses and breweries, was not determined as it had been before the mid-1880s by brewers buying cautiously out of profits and occasionally on modest mortgage, because the rapid application of limited liability to the industry after 1886 completely transformed the finances of the larger, more adventurous breweries.

Until the mid-1880s, breweries, with their tight family control and very adequate finances, were not amongst the front runners of those firms which sought the benefits of limited liability. The few breweries which had done so in the early 1880s, like the Lion, Bow, City of London and Burton Brewery companies, had been notable neither for their repute nor their success. When, however, conditions of prosperity returned to the industry in 1886, the public conversion of Guinness late in that year completely transformed the situation. This £6 million issue was over-subscribed several times. Suddenly the biggest brewers, company promoters and financiers realised that the flotation of companies could yield big capital gains. The boom was on. In 1886 alone, twenty-eight firms with a capital of £9.5 million changed from partnership to public company status. Within four years no fewer than 200 breweries had taken the benefits of the Companies' Act, including such leaders as Ind Coope (1886), Allsopp (1887), Whitbread (1888) and Courage (1889), although little more than a third of these were public joint-stock companies with entries in the Stock Exchange's breweries listing. Even in 1900 out of 270 brewing companies with limited liability only seventy-one had made a partial issue of ordinary and preference shares.

No historian of the industry has argued that the change in status of brewing partnerships substantially altered either their ownership or management. With the smallest number of exceptions like Allsopp and Ind Coope, cases in which their flotations went sadly awry, the old brewing families retained their control of affairs. But limited liability, making possible the issue of large numbers of debenture and preference shares, allowed those firms in London, Burton, and the provinces that had owned few or no public houses to partake in the intense race for public houses after 1886 at an undreamt-of pace. For the London and Burton breweries this was particularly important. For the former, the severe contraction of trade in the early 1880s had led publicans into heavy debt and the pressures this placed on brewers' loan accounts, together with the need to expensively modernise the great city drinking 'palaces', and secure a tie that excluded Burton beers, were major considerations in a shift in policy which encouraged the larger

London brewers to convert burgeoning loan-tie mortgages into substantial leaseholds. In the capital, at the height of the 'Brewers' Wars' between 1895 and 1902, some 500 houses a year were acquired in this way. Public house prices were driven sky-high. London brewers were borrowing extensively by debenture issue to keep abreast of their rivals. When Barclay Perkins went public in 1896 they offered a debenture issue of £1.2 million to allow them to enter, rather belatedly, the public house market. Likewise Bass, on a similar mission, issued £1.8 million in debentures and preference shares during 1888 to 1889, and Allsopp between 1897 and 1900 increased their share issue by an extraordinary £3.25 million to buy houses at prices which *The Economist* considered 'insane'. Elsewhere provincial breweries were expanding with similar, if smaller, debenture issues. By 1900 it is reckoned some 260 firms had issued a colossal £185 million worth of debentures and shares, largely to finance the acquisition of public houses. On the other hand there were more cautious firms, like Georges and Greene King, who expanded their tied empires appreciably – the latter from 141 in 1887 to 378 houses by 1902 – by regular purchases out of reserves with only minimal debenture issues. Possibly, many smaller breweries increased their holdings of public houses in this way.

It was the scale on which breweries borrowed in the 1890s that really determined their profitability after 1900. Then all breweries were ground between declining consumption and, after 1906, hostile government legislation. With over-capacity and no way of increasing prices, breweries entered a period of unprecedented difficulty. Some survived these years with relative ease, whilst others drifted into liquidation or at best paid their shareholders beggarly dividends of one or two per cent until conditions improved after 1912. There were other factors besides the financial ones: the London trade was more competitive than ever and Burton brewers found any headway both in the capital and provinces more and more difficult. Even though Allsopp's management was poor there was truth in their contention that an almost completely tied trade placed restrictions on their beers which drove down their sales year after year in the 1900s. But the real clue to brewing profitability after 1900 comes from a consideration of the debt brewers had taken on so readily between 1886 and 1902. When companies were profitable, and there were notable examples of these after 1900, the situation invariably reflected their modest contraction of debt in the 1890s and the tightness of their managements in trimming brewing costs and running economically their tied estates in these difficult years.

During the nineteenth century the actual method of brewing changed very little. The traditional materials of water, malt, hops and yeast continued to be combined with great skill in the time-honoured way of centuries. Brewers were conservative men each carefully preserving, often very secretively, established, empirical practices which had been handed down to them. Of course, there were changes at all levels. With materials, sugar began to be substituted for the use of malt after 1880, allowing brewers to achieve better results when barley qualities were poor and released less saccharine in their conversion. Had barley prices not been so low between 1880 and 1914 the use of sugar might well have been higher. Hopping rates also declined by some forty per cent in these years, partly because of changing tastes, partly because brewers were seeking to reduce operating costs. Although these trends will show in the stock books and calculations of brewers, a more obvious change was in the way most brewers introduced machinery. Brewing patents grew very rapidly in the half century of great prosperity after 1830, and by the 1870s the brewing journals were enthusing about the number of new machines available to aid every stage of production. In addition to the widespread use of steam power in heating, pumping and lifting materials, the principal inventions really centred on the problem of cooling worts and beers. There are countless examples of refrigerating plant, attemperators, and ice machines intended to improve the manufacture and storage of beer throughout the year. Basically, by 1900 their use allowed brewers to achieve a rapid turnover of large quantities of weaker 'running' beers, instead of the old vatted 'stock' beers and porters of the earlier nineteenth century. There were other important innovations which aided the powered mashing of malt in the 1830s and, especially important, the improved bottling of beer after the mid-1880s by pasteurisation and filtration. During the boom of the 1860s and 1870s and again in the late 1880s and 1890s many breweries were rebuilt on the up-to-date 'tower' principle that facilitated the production of the new, 'running' ales. They contained the latest machinery often fitted by one of the leading brewing engineering firms, like Adlams of Bristol. Barnard's well-known four-volume *Noted Breweries of Great Britain and Ireland* (1889-1891) is a celebration of their construction.

When historians of brewing turn from a consideration of materials and technology to the question of how far the industry was affected by scientific advances in the half-century before 1914, they face a more difficult task. Although the brewing journals are in no doubt that the industry was revolutionised in this field during these years, although the work of Pasteur on the 'infection' of beers and Hanson on pure yeasts was of the utmost importance, although the biggest breweries like Bass, Allsopp, Worthington and Guinness employed chemists whose findings were significant, although The Institute of Brewing was set up in 1886 to disseminate much of this research through its journal and meetings, it is unclear how far the average brewery discussed and applied these findings. There was an indifference to science in a conservative industry and a feeling that brewers knew their own business best. More generally, the readiness of brewers to adopt the latest technology on the one hand, with an inclination to dismiss the latest scientific findings in their field as inappropriate on the other, is an interesting dimension in the important discussion about the quality of late Victorian businessmen.

The inter-war years

The years which stretched from the outbreak of the First World War to the late 1950s were generally difficult ones for brewers. They were marked by three key features: an almost continuous decline in beer production; an accelerated amalgamation of brewing firms; and a predilection for government to tax the industry far more severely than it had done before

1914. As usual, relentless general factors differed in their impact, both in their incidence for individual firms and in their uniformity across a long forty-five-year span. In effect there were four quite distinct periods – 1914-20, 1920-39, 1939-45 and 1945-59 – although the variation of regional unemployment between the wars and the severity of government restriction between 1945 and 1953 undermines their cohesiveness.

When war was declared in August 1914 few brewers can have imagined that it would transform their industry so completely. It did so largely in terms of government interference and restriction. Lloyd George, in a string of celebrated speeches in the spring of 1915, blamed the shortage of munitions upon the brewers and 'the lure of drink'. It was, he thundered, 'doing us more damage in the war than all the German submarines put together'. By late 1915 the Central Control Board directed the production, sale, and distribution of alcohol more completely than at any other period in its history. Opening hours were slashed, the brewing industry was threatened with nationalisation. Direct control of the drink trade was worked out in three areas, although it has always been known, from its chief centre, as the 'Carlisle Experiment'. There were attempts to encourage the sale of food and light beers on licensed premises. Duties per standard barrel were increased almost seven times to fifty shillings in 1918 and doubled again by 1920. The industry, with its work-force depleted, reeled. The industry's output figures underline the point most forcibly: expressed in standard barrels they declined from 35,951,000 in 1913 to 13,012,000 in 1919. Of course, the fall in bulk barrels was nothing like so appreciable because standard gravities fell from the pre-war average of 1053° to 1030°. Roughly, brewers were producing two-thirds of the bulk output with one-third of the raw materials.

Yet, as with farmers, the later war-years and immediate post-war period was a good one for brewers. They were allowed to advance prices significantly as duties rose sharply, and since an Excess Profits Duty was introduced rather late and less tightly than in 1939, brewers enjoyed extremely healthy profits on their reduced sales. Their weak, characterless beers sold readily. At the height of this prosperity between 1917 and 1920, menaced by threats of nationalisation and realising the benefits of rationalisation in a contracting market, many brewers eagerly bought up those competitors who were prepared to realise their family firms for capital gain. As a consequence the number of common brewers contracted sharply by thirty-five per cent from 4,512 in 1910 to 2,914 in 1920.

In 1920 these enlarged breweries, which now had an average output of over 12,000 barrels each, looked forward to a return to normality, the end of the detested Central Control Board, and a diminution in duties. The relief did not materialise. Although controls were wound up (but the draconian wartime licensing restrictions were continued), duties remained high throughout the inter-war years with only temporary periods of respite after sharp rises in the early 1920s and again in 1931. Most worryingly, consumption declined to 1934 and then made only the most modest recovery. The figures are set out in Table 3.

As in the period before 1914 changing social habits provide a better explanation of these figures than the temperance drive, although it was not, together with the Government's posturing on nationalisation and further licensing restriction, finally recognised as a spent force until the early 1930s. Workers in the inter-war years, especially the young, appeared to spend increasing amounts of their pay packets (although real wages fell between 1920 and 1923) on a variety of alternatives – the cinema (at its peak in the 1930s forty per cent of the population went weekly), radios, football pools and an increasing range of recreational pastimes. These important trends, difficult to measure precisely but recognised by all brewers as making considerable inroads on the old working-class public-house culture, were reinforced by the high level of unemployment which was such a general feature of the inter-war economy. Sharp upturns during the periods 1920 to 1923 and 1929 to 1933 account for the worst years for brewers. In some areas, like

Table 3
United Kingdom beer output and consumption, 1910-39

Years	Beer output (million standard barrels of 1055°)	Consumption per head (gallons)
1910-14	34.1	26.9
1915-19	22.7	16.5
1920-24	22.3	16.4
1925-29	20.3	16.3
1930-34	16.6	13.0
1935-39	16.9	13.2

Source: B R Mitchell and P Deane, Abstract of British Historical Statistics (1962), p. 253.

South Wales, the North-East and Glasgow, breweries were hit hard. Hancock in Cardiff and Hammonds in Bradford paid no dividends in the 1930s. But no breweries escaped a diminution in sales between 1931 and 1933. The other factor, which required careful handling, was that beer prices were too high. Brewers had to demonstrate that big peacetime advances in duty between 1918 and 1920 and in 1931, when they advanced to £6 14s per standard barrel and accounted for almost sixty per cent of the price of beer, meant that they were unable to reduce prices although raw material costs were low after 1920. Any worthwhile reduction, they argued, would have wiped out their fragile profitability. Only in 1933 was relief at last given when the Government completely reformed the duty system and further encouraged the production of weaker beers by charging a minimal duty on a bulk barrel of 1027° gravity with proportional rises for every further two degrees in strength. Beer never reached anything like its old pre-war strengths. In 1939 average gravity was 1041°; and charges and convictions for drunkenness declined across the inter-war years. Britain was, as Lord Woolton the Minister of Food described it in 1940, 'a temperate nation.'

How did brewers react to these changed conditions? The way forward for those that weathered the storm was to do so by amalgamation. Many family firms which faced the usual demographic, managerial, and taxation problems simply put their breweries on the market. Invariably, competitors and survivors were approached informally by sellers in the old gentlemanly way of the industry. But the pressures were real and the numbers of brewers fell very sharply by over seventy per cent between 1920 and 1940. Firms grew by purchase and amalgamation from the great Allsopp and Ind Coope merger of 1934 (both had been active purchasers in the 1920s), through regional brewers like Simonds, Ansell, Vaux and Walker Cain, to quite small ones like Charles Wells in Bedford and Wells & Winch in Biggleswade. Indeed it is reckoned that almost every one of the 500 or so active breweries in 1940 had been involved in at least one merger or purchase arrangement. Although there was this disposition to create larger, more viable firms, brewers had to activate a development strategy usually based upon the bottling of beer and the tighter management of their tied estates.

In terms of brewing technology and investment the principal change from the supply side centred upon the large-scale bottling of beer. The pioneering stages had been worked out in the twenty years before 1914. But after 1920 demand grew rapidly. Again it was the result of subtle social changes, and whatever its causes, it became much the brightest aspect of brewing profitability after the early 1920s. All brewers now had to attempt to bottle a range of well-conditioned, bright beers. This was, of course, a further threat to the smaller brewers who could not find, or justify, the considerable investment for a bottling line. Moreover, Guinness, Bass, Worthington and Watney led a number of London and Burton brewers in bottling beer for a countrywide market, reinforcing their ventures by a national advertising campaign. After 1933 some of these firms, in contrast to their experiences before 1914, became highly profitable, as did those regional brewers away from the worst areas of unemployment who owned and had improved their tied estates. This switch to bottled beer was facilitated by transport changes. In the early 1920s fleets of lorries, themselves good advertisements, replaced the large number of dray horses all breweries had employed until the First World War. Except for town deliveries, horses, the symbol of the old brewing world, disappeared very quickly.

The other major preoccupation of brewers was in the improvement of their houses. Not much, except the building of some splendid pubs in the largest cities before 1914 and by Mitchell & Butler and Ansell in the Birmingham area, had been achieved in this respect. Even after 1920 improvement was a delicate task. Licensing magistrates controlled the process, and until the fall in drunkenness statistics became obvious in the late 1920s, they could be hostile. But brewers realised that to attract drinkers they had to improve facilities; the old spartan, tap room layout of many Victorian public houses was swept away to create more space and seating. In tourist areas, and especially in the prosperous south-east, breweries like Benskins of Watford and Whitbread prided themselves on building capacious, comfortable houses for the motoring public, forcing competitors into improving their own tied property. Keeping a works department going, devising a regular programme of updating were expensive but necessary items for all but the smallest and most vulnerable breweries. Allied to improvement were changes in the running of public houses. Direct management had been introduced during the First World War, both in Carlisle and by Mitchell & Butler in Birmingham. After 1920 many breweries followed their lead and turned over their profitable houses to direct management. The movement was not so controversial as it became in the 1960s because most breweries did not pursue the policy aggressively and because many tenants appeared to have preferred a direct wage in difficult times. An additional feature of the inter-war period is the rise of the club trade. Again club licences were well in evidence before 1914, but after 1920 they grew so rapidly that they almost replaced the contracting numbers of full licences. By 1935 there were 15,657 registered clubs. Brewers were suspicious of them, but they found, much as they disliked their competition, that they were forced into making loans to them in exchange for the supply of beer.

The Second World War offered a very different prospect from the First World War for brewers. With the sharp decline in consumption and drunkenness across the 1920s and 1930s, gone was any government attempt to restrict output as in the 1914 to 1919 period. Of course, there were brewing material restrictions and shortages, but bulk barrelage in fact increased by a quarter between 1938 and 1944. Brewers simply brewed a weak, undistinguished beer and, as during the First World War, they emerged from it in 1945 enjoying a healthy profitability. The years from 1945 to 1959 were no brighter for brewers than had been the prospects in the 1920s. Demand fell slowly year after year to 1959, when it was twenty-seven per cent below its 1945 level. The production figures for 1945 to 1988 are set out overleaf in Table 4.

High levels of duty (not relaxed until the 1959 budget) and taxation bit hard into profits, and the brewers' constant need to update their tied properties and breweries, after years of wartime neglect and severe building restrictions to 1953, meant that they had problems in generating sufficient capital to carry out their programmes of improvement. In these conditions of over-capacity, brewers continued to rationalise in the time-honoured way of acquiring additional breweries. The number of active brewing companies declined by over a half between 1940 and 1960. By the latter date there were only 247. Invariably breweries were bought or merged by the old insider's route between gentlemen. Of course many breweries and pubs with poor trade were closed, but before 1959 there were no contested takeovers. Within this pattern of development after the late 1940s, the national brewers – Guinness, Watney Combe Reid, Bass Worthington, Ind Coope & Allsopp, Charrington, Whitbread and Truman, Hanbury & Buxton – did best. Aggressively marketing bottled beers, they penetrated deeper into what free trade there was; they acquired breweries; and they made reciprocal trading agreements everywhere. Even so, the degree of concentration within the industry in the early 1950s was not large; the six biggest breweries owned only sixteen per cent of licensed premises; there were still 200 firms owning fewer than a hundred public houses each (the average of these was as low as thirty-four houses and six off-licences apiece). By the late 1950s as some

Table 4
Beer produced in the United Kingdom, 1945-1988
(in million bulk barrels)

Year ending 31 March		Year ending 31 March	
1945	31.0	1967	29.9
1946	32.7	1968	30.1
1947	29.2	1969	30.8
1948	30.0	1970	32.0
1949	27.0	1971	33.3
1950	25.8	1972	34.1
1951	24.8	1973	34.7
1952	24.7	1974	37.1
1953	24.4	1975	37.5
1954	24.2	1976	37.8
1955	23.6	1977	39.1
1956	24.1	1978	39.5
1957	24.2	1979	40.5
1958	24.2	1980	39.6
1959	23.4	1981	37.7
1960	25.4	1982	36.5
1961	26.3	1983	36.8
1962	27.4	1984	36.7
1963	27.1	1985	36.4
1964	28.2	1986	36.3
1965	28.7	1987	36.6
1966	29.1	1988	36.7

Source: The Brewers' Society, *UK Statistical Handbook* (1988).

shrewd, non-brewing financiers realised, the industry was ripe for rapid rationalisation.

The decades of change
Since 1960 the brewing industry has been transformed: in its structure; in its products; and in its functions. Structurally the industry altered very rapidly after 1959. Suddenly, brewers pushed along by financiers like Sir Charles Clore realised that the retailing outlets of breweries were grossly undervalued, often at historic cost, in their accounts. To protect the industry from outside marauders truly national brewing firms had to be created quickly. Six great conglomerates came to dominate the industry by the mid-1960s. Each of them, except Whitbread, grew rapidly by merger and acquisition in an extraordinarily competitive rationalisation, principally between 1959 and 1963. In addition, there was the great Guinness firm which retained a healthy share of the market without tied outlets. The position at the end of the movement in the mid-1970s is given in Table 5.

The industry had concentrated so quickly, not in comparison with levels

Table 5
Beer market shares and ownership of on-licensed premises in the mid-1970s

Company	No. of UK breweries (1976)	Share of beer sales (1976) %	No. of on-licensed premises (inc. clubs and hotels) (1974)	% of total
Bass Charrington	12	20	9,256	8.2
Allied Breweries	7	17	7,665	6.8
Whitbread	19	13	7,865	6.9
Watney/Grand Metropolitan Hotels	8	12	5,946	5.2
Scottish & Newcastle	3	11	1,678	1.5
Courage/Imperial Group	8	9	5,921	5.2
Guinness	1	9	—	—
Others	89	9	13,800	12.2
Free trade	—	—	61,498	54.0
Total	147	100	113,629	100.0

Source: Hawkins and Pass, *Brewing Industry,* pp. 79, 82.
Note: In 1989 Bass owned 7,300 public houses and restaurants, Allied 6,600, Whitbread 6,500, Grand Metropolitan 6,100, Courage 5,100 and Scottish & Newcastle 2,300. Together they produced seventy-five per cent of UK beer output, and owned seventy-five per cent of its tied houses (Source: *Financial Times,* 22 March 1989).

in brewing abroad, but in terms of its own evolution, that there have been a series of government and European Economic Community inquiries examining aspects of forward integration (i.e. the uniquely strong links between production and retailing) and prices over twenty years. Most recently, in March 1989, the Monopolies Commission recommended that, in order to stimulate competition, no brewer should own more than 2,000 public houses each. In fact, regional and local brewers that have survived – about eighty are active in the late 1980s – have done well. Encouraged by the Campaign for Real Ale (CAMRA), they have successfully marketed their cask beers since the early 1970s, when the national breweries went headlong into keg and lager production. It is in the manufacture of these – lager absorbed more than forty per cent of beer consumption by the mid-1980s – that the nationals, taking advantage of packaging, dispensing, and distribution innovations, led 'the beer revolution' of the 1960s and 1970s. Nowhere was this more evident than in the expansion of lager brewing. Technical advances in brewing were matched by those in marketing and investment to promote nationally the Harp, Carling Black Label, Skol,

Heineken and Carlsberg brands. All these changes required a heavy investment which all except the largest regional breweries failed to match. They were enacted against the background of changing consumer tastes and the rapid expansion of the market between 1960 and 1979 (see Table 4). National advertising, chiefly on television, promoted leading brands of brewery-conditioned beers. It allowed the 'big six' to make deep incursions into the free trade which grew rapidly after the Licensing Act of 1961 opened up supermarket and off-licence sales. Between 1950 and 1980 the number of off-licences in the United Kingdom increased by sixty-four per cent.

The functions of the traditional brewers have also changed rapidly. For centuries they concentrated upon producing beer and, since the 1870s, selling it through tied outlets. But after 1960, with rapidly rising living standards, brewers realised that they could generate a far better return on this key investment by supplying food and leisure facilities. As the new and refurbished managed houses acquired these functions they became no longer primarily outlets for beer. In the hotel and off-licence trades brewers moved with similar alacrity after 1960.

At its peak in 1979 United Kingdom beer production was 40.5 million bulk barrels, having grown from 24.8 million bulk barrels in 1951. A sudden downturn in the market occurred in 1980 and during that year production figures fell appreciably for the first time for almost twenty years. Since 1982 annual production figures have been running at approximately ten per cent less than the 1979 high point. This fall in beer consumption was seen by the National Economic Development Office to be linked with such adverse economic influences as inflationary pressure on discretionary income, increases in the price of beer in real terms and unemployment. It was also noted that beer consumption in other countries had also been declining as consumer tastes changed. The resultant over-capacity in the British industry (it was calculated in early 1989 that breweries in aggregate were only producing seventy per cent of their optimum capacity), with some breweries operating a five day fortnight, has led to further takeovers during the mid-1980s.

These changes, momentous since the 1950s in terms of size and technology, have brought us a long way from the industry of 1750. The industry, and this is true of the individual brewing firm also, has been rather neglected by historians, certainly in comparison with coal, iron and steel, and cotton. Perhaps the fact that it possesses an essentially conservative form of industrial capitalism and carried 'the demon drink' stigma, which no Nonconformist or socialist historian could avoid, explains its comparative neglect. But it has been and still is a major industry in the United Kingdom, as well as being the third largest brewing industry in the world, and study of its history is highly instructive in many ways about British attitudes and traditions.

Richard Wilson

This article first appeared in *The Brewing Industry: A Guide to Historical Records,* edited by Lesley Richmond and Alison Turton, Manchester University Press, 1990. It is reprinted here by kind permission of the author and publishers.

TODAY ST. ALBANS, TOMORROW THE WORLD

IT IS LIKE saying grace. In the wine cellars of Baron Bachofen von Echt, under his *schloss* at Nussdorf, on the edge of the Vienna woods, I have raised a glass of "Sir Henry's" dry stout, brewed on the premises, and said a silent prayer of thanks to the Campaign for Real Ale.

Under a windmill in Amsterdam, at the Egg Brewery, I have sampled an abbey-style ale called Ostrich and entertained the same thought.

Over *une verre d'ambrée* at Les Brasseurs, in Lille, I have proferred my thanks before tucking into *coq à la bière*. Likewise before a glass of St Ambroise, in Montreal.

An unfiltered, Vienna-style lager at Zip City, downstairs from the old offices of the National Temperance Society, in the Flat Iron district of Manhattan? Zip City's literary debt is to Sinclair Lewis, but there would have been no such brewpubs, lager or not, without the inspiration of the Campaign for Real Ale. An "Irish" Ale at the Goose Island brewpub, in Chicago, or a "Scottish" one in Sherlock's Home (in the suburbs of Minneapolis? Great Scot, Watson!). Come to that, an Irish Ale at Big Rock in Calgary or a Scottish one at Grant's, in Yakima (the kind of town where they ask you to check your gun as well as your hat), in the Cascade Mountains. How can I, or they, ever repay our debts to CAMRA?

Is there no end to these delights? How about an Oyster Stout at the Pike Place Brewery, in Seattle; a Boysenberry Wheat Beer, at Rogue River, in Ashland, Oregon; a Big Foot Barley Wine, at Sierra Nevada, in Chico, California? Thank you, CAMRA. Thank you very much indeed.

I have sipped a fruity, Düsseldorf-style *Altbier* made by Sapporo, and served in the Lion Brasserie, under the Komatsu building in the Ginza district of Tokyo; a maltier interpretation of the same style at Suntory's experimental brewery in the horse-racing town of Fuchu City; and a rather caramelly version at Kirin's Spring Valley brewpub in Yokohama. Do the astonishingly skilled brewers of Japan know they owe a debt to CAMRA? Some do. You would be surprised.

In Melbourne, there was a wonderfully creamy milk stout, inappropriately called Razorback, at the Geebung Polo Club; near Canberra, a much drier, thinner, stout made by Father Michael O'Halloran, a catholic priest, at the Old Goulburn brewery; at Picton, on the road to Sydney, the silky Burragorang Bock produced by a brewer called Deo Gratias Lule, born in Kenya but educated in malty magic in Edinburgh. Do I thank CAMRA once more? Yes , I do. Let me explain why.

When CAMRA was born, breweries were closing not only in Britain but also in the United States and most other parts of the developed world. The surviving breweries were making blander and blander beers, and fewer of them, not just in England, Wales and Scotland, but almost everywhere else. Since prohibition in the United States, two world wars, and the growth of mass-marketing in the 1950s and 1960s, people had believed that a brewery was something that closed. They had convinced themselves that bland beer was inevitable.

The founders of CAMRA set out to save traditional breweries and beers, not to inspire new ones, but that was the effect of their efforts. They concerned themselves only with Britain, but their inspiration spread far and wide.

Within three or four years of CAMRA's birth in 1971, new breweries were opening in Britain. Soon afterwards, they were starting all over the developed world.

The oldest type of brewery, that attached to a pub, had in Britain diminished in number to four, but scores have opened since then. Some have closed after a year or two, but there are today 50 or 60 in Britain. Inspired by that revival, Bert Grant (today a legend in American beer) opened his brewpub in the old opera house at Yakima, Washington. Down the coast, a kettle was fired in a 100-year-old saloon in the appropriately-named town of Hopland, in Mendocino County, California. There are today about 150 brewpubs in the United States.

The other category of new small brewery is the tiny, free-standing, business. This is smaller than an old-established local or regional brewery, and more likely to produce speciality beers. Without the climate created by CAMRA, would Peter Austin have come out of retirement to establish the pioneering Ringwood micro-brewery (famous for its Old Thumper)? I do not believe so for a moment. Austin went on to help establish micro-breweries elsewhere in Europe, all over North America, and even in China, in the 1980s. Having girdled the New World, the movement came back to the Old, to Belgium and The Netherlands, and even to Germany, where a new generation of brewpubs joined the hundreds of long-established ones.

At one of the earliest Great British Beer Festivals, I encountered a man named Jack McAuliffe, who had been in Britain with the United States Navy. He had been inspired by the Campaign for Real Ale, and was in the process of starting America's first micro-brewery, in Sonoma, California. He proved to be ahead of his time, but today there almost 100 micros in the U.S.

At another Great British Beer Festival, I was approached by Gordon Bowker, one of the Berkeley generation of the 1960s. He had helped start an alternative newspaper, and a "gourmet" coffee-roasting company, both in Seattle. He had sought me out to see whether I thought a micro-brewery would work in Seattle. I hope I encouraged him, though my memories are fogged by the beer we enjoyed together. The brewery he subsequently helped found, Red Hook, is today one of the most successful in America, and Seattle the country's new beer capital.

We are talking here about inspiration, not imitation. The man who runs the Red Door bar in Seattle may, like me, be a Lithuanian Yorkshireman, but his establishment sells fine (yes, cask-conditioned) beers that are definitely New American in their character.

Like the best of Britain's local, regional and national brewers, their counterparts in the United States (and other developed nations) have begun to offer a wider range of beers, including some genuine specialities. The country's oldest brewery, in Pottsville, Pennsylvania, once seemed set to close, but today is prospering on the success of its celebrated Porter. Even the country's biggest single brewery plant, Coors, in Golden, Colorado, makes a creditable Vienna-style lager, called Winterfest, as a seasonal special.

CAMRA's Great British Beer Festival itself has been an inspiration, too. In the early 1980s, a group of enthusiasts in Boulder, Colorado, started a similar Great American Beer Festival, open to brewpubs, micros, locals, regionals and national brewers. The festival soon moved to the bigger city of Denver, and has grown every year since. It is for the moment a two-day festival, but on those evenings it is as packed as its longer British inspiration, and it offers a greater diversity of beers.

CAMRA's monthly tabloid "What's Brewing" has inspired similar papers in Baltimore, New York, Minneapolis, Denver and San Francisco. There have even been several efforts to launch glossy magazines for beer-lovers, in Italy, France, Belgium, Britain itself, the United States, Canada and Australia. CAMRA's annual *Good Beer Guide* has inspired more modest booklets in the U.S., and there is currently one in preparation in Japan.

Without the celebration of beer by CAMRA, journalists, authors and television programme-makers would never have been emboldened to discuss in such detail their favourite products, nor editors accepted their essays. There is still less writing on beer than there is on wine, but you can nonetheless find the two alongside one another in some of the Saturday papers every other week. There is now such an animal as a beer-writer, not only in Britain but also in the United States, Australia and elsewhere.

On my own travels in search of beer, I constantly meet brewers who have visited Britain to sample real ale, see how it is made, and make a pilgrimage to CAMRA's offices in the unlikely location of St Albans. When we greet one another, it is almost as though there should be some secret handshake. We feel as though we are in a resistance movement, fighting against Fear of Flavour. By the time the night is out, we will have commiserated over blandness in beer, bread, cheese...The fight is against a bland quality of life.

Many beer-lovers in the United States and elsewhere join CAMRA just so that they can stand up and be counted. There is little direct benefit for them. Attempts are being made to start something similar, but of more practical local application, in the U.S. There is a sister organisation in Canada, and there are counterparts in Scandinavia, The Netherlands and Belgium.

Then again, I meet new brewers and beer-lovers who have recently jumped on the dray, and who have no idea where all this started. "We've got all these great new breweries. They make fantastic beers!" enthuses a trucker in Tallahassee, a dentist in Dayton, a surfer in San Diego. "Do you have anything like that in Europe?" I bite my tongue and smilingly nod assent. Four Britons started the whole thing, back in 1971.

Sure, the elements were universal: leisure was on the increase, and some found it in a new appreciation of food and drink; people were beginning to travel more, and discover the tastes of other nations; that new perspective also gave them a more appreciative view of their own heritage; conservation of architecture had spread to other aspects of life; consumers sought variety; the more discerning wanted authenticity, and demanded to know how a product was made, and what it contained; for some, small was beautiful...

Many of us felt these impulses, but we thought nothing could be done, until the Famous Four proved us wrong. It was only then that we joined the battle.

Those friends who do not understand chide me: 'You used to write about more serious things; now it's all beer." Journalists imagine they can change the world. The founders of CAMRA did.

Michael Jackson

FOUNDING FATHERS

OVER THE PAST twenty-one years, I have become fed up to the bladder of people introducing themselves as founder members of CAMRA or as friends of someone's cousin who established the Campaign single-handedly.

These bores first came to my notice when I was sheltering from the wind and rain in a keg-only pub in Berkhamsted while on a canal holiday in Hertfordshire in 1977. A drunk who worked in a boatyard began to regale the sparsely populated bar with tales of how he and his friends had founded CAMRA at Manchester University in 1968. As he wolfed down the Double Diamond, he became so loud that one of my companions, altogether more athletic than the rest of us, asked him to pipe down and told him that in any case this bloke Hardman here was a *genuine* founder member of the Campaign.

The drunk threatened to 'do a Vienna' on my mate but before we could discover what sort of pain or pleasure that involved, he was evicted by the publican and told not to return until he was sober.

Shortly afterwards, when I was working on the *Evening Standard* in London – where the lunch break was from 11 a.m. to noon – I was busy organising an opening-time trip to the nearest Burton Ale pub when a newcomer announced that he could tell us a thing or two about real ale because his father was a founder member of CAMRA. It turned out that the father in question had once written an article about the Campaign in a now-defunct magazine, but even after my colleagues had pointed out the true founder member in their midst, the son persisted with his claim.

Over the next few years, bogus founders appeared everywhere. Then, a few years ago, I stopped meeting them. They had, thankfully, gone to ground. Or so I thought, until earlier this year, a cutting from the *Coventry Evening Telegraph* suddenly came my way via the unlikely route of Sydney and Munich.

Here was an article "by Steve Evans, founder member of CAMRA." Mr Evans entertained his readers with the tale of how he, Bill Mellor and some fellow called Hardiman (sic), who was balding and bespectacled, had launched the Campaign in Nuneaton in 1970. Well, Mr Evans, I have too *much* hair rather than too little, I have never worn glasses in my life, I had never set foot in Nuneaton until 1972 (more of which later) and, what's more, I wouldn't know you from Adam. For you, then, and for your many fellow imposters, here is the truth about the birth of CAMRA.

A pint of better beer?
Bill Mellor, Graham Lees and I were journalists from the Manchester and Liverpool area. Jim Makin, who worked in the company secretary's department at a brewery in Salford, was a life-long friend of Lees. All of us were under twenty-five and fond of a few pints. The first time the four of us came together was in March 1971, when we gathered in Chester on the evening before we were to fly off to Ireland for a seven-day boozing holiday

organised by Lees. As we traipsed from pub to pub and finally to the compulsory Indian restaurant, we developed a consensus of complaint about the lousy quality of much of the beer we had drunk. 'Too fizzy,' said Mellor. 'No character,' said Makin. 'Too dear,' said Lees. 'Tastes sickly,' said I.

We arrived in Dublin on Sunday lunchtime still moaning about the previous night's ale, but buoyed up by the promise of a trip to the Guinness brewery at St James's Gate on the Monday. We did our homework on the Sunday by downing as much Guinness as the licensing laws allowed and we were in much better mood when Monday came. Nevertheless, we had noted that the Irish ale – generally Smithwick's and sold in bars that advertised Ted Castle's Best Coal – was even worse than what we had found in Chester.

The murmurings of a campaign for better beer had begun. Lees was in favour of calling the stuff we liked 'ale'; 'beer,' he argued, was the word for the southern rubbish that was being foisted on us by the brewers. Makin said ale and beer were the same thing, but he did prefer the word 'ale.' So did Mellor and I.

The idea of the acronym CAMRA came to me while we were walking across the Guinness brewery yard. Mellor and Lees were trying to work out how to take pictures with a camera borrowed from one of their newspaper colleagues. 'CAMERA…Campaign for…something…Ale,' I announced to an unimpressed Makin. 'Restoration of Ale,' suggested Mellor. 'No, Revitalisation of Ale,' Lees insisted. 'It's more of a laugh.'

Lees had summed it up. The idea of forming a campaign to improve beer *was* a laugh. We were playing at secret societies. The idea stuck, however, and on the evening of 16 March, we held the first meeting of our new brotherhood, with no inkling of the far-reaching effects that our actions would one day have on the pattern of drinking and brewing throughout Britain.

We had driven out along the Kerry coast to what Mellor reckoned was the westernmost pub in Europe. It was called Patrick O'Neill's and only the four of us and Mr O'Neill's mother could speak English. We elected ourselves as officers of the new campaign: Lees was to be secretary, Makin treasurer, Mellor events organiser and Hardman chairman. We settled on Campaign for the Revitalisation of Ale and decided boldly to drop the E from CAMERA as it seemed to stand for nothing. CAMRA was born, with no clear aims, no battle plan and no membership to speak of.

Almost a year later, our Irish holiday now a fond memory, Lees and I were doing the rounds of the pubs of Chester again when Lees became uncharacteristically serious. 'You know, Hardman,' he said with wrinkled brow and screwed-up eyes. 'We should get this CAMRA business going as a proper consumer campaign instead of just buggering about singing We're Only Here for the Ale.'

Lees had already recruited a dozen souls to the cause – whatever the cause was – by producing a Christmas card with what he himself later described as a daft doggerel, complete with an overdose of capital letters:

> Whether In City Bar You Sup,
> Or In Village Vault You Get Tanked Up,

Be On Your Guard Against Bad Ale,
Or You'll Never Live To Tell The Tale
Of CAMRA.

Lees had unilaterally decided to get membership cards printed, too, and flogged them off at five pence a time, which gave the fledgling Campaign liquid assets of sixty pence, though there is no record of this vast sum ever having been passed to Makin, the elected treasurer.

Lees's suggestion that CAMRA should now pass itself off as a serious consumer organisation stunned me at first, but he persisted and we called the first annual meeting of the Campaign to coincide roughly with the anniversary of our trip to Ireland. The first AGM was held at the Rose Inn, Coton Road, Nuneaton, because that's where Mellor now lived and because it was considered a convenient location as Lees and I now lived in the London area and Makin was still in Salford. The meeting was a drunken affair, attended by about 20 friends of Lees and Mellor, and I incurred the wrath of the licensees by constantly banging a glass on the table when calling for order, but we did elect a national executive and adopted a written constitution peppered with childish references to 'slutchers' and 'slutching,' as secret-society synonyms for drinkers and drink. Later, and without consulting anyone, Lees and I drastically edited this document, and altered the minutes of the AGM accordingly, not only to delete the embarrassing phraseology but also to make the Campaign's objectives clearer and its administration tighter.

CAMRA was now launched, thanks to the vision of Lees, who went back to his bedsitter in St Albans to keep the membership records in a now legendary shoebox. Mellor took little further active part in CAMRA, except to suggest *What's Brewing* as the title of our new monthly newspaper, and Makin dropped out because of his position in the brewing industry. The national executive we had elected at the Rose fell apart after a few months, but the Campaign had begun to attract some powerful and knowledgeable allies, who had been waiting for years, unbeknown to us, for just such an organisation to come along.

We now had people of the calibre of Christopher Hutt, author of *Death of the English Pub* and later to become CAMRA's second chairman; Frank Baillie, author of *The Beer Drinker's Companion;* John Green, who took over as secretary from Lees and later became CAMRA's first full-time employee; Terry Pattinson, an industrial correspondent with the *Daily Express* and now with the *Daily Mirror;* and John Hanscomb, a veritable fount of knowledge who edited the *Good Beer Guide* voluntarily before it became necessary for the job to be handled by paid staff.

We called a special general meeting, again in Nuneaton, to reconstitute the Campaign and to get these stalwarts elected to the executive. It was poorly attended but it was the final launching pad for the campaign that was to prove the cynics wrong. The Campaign for the Revitalisation of Ale outgrew our wildest expectations within a few months and by the time the second annual meeting was held in London in 1973, there were more than 1,000 members on the books. The only barrier to further growth, it seemed, was the title of the Campaign itself, which was proving to be a mouthful even when we were sober.

'Real ale' was a phrase coined in early issues of *What's Brewing* and was becoming widely used to describe traditionally brewed and properly served draught beer, but it took the genius of Peter Linley, one of the Campaign's pioneers in the Midlands, to realise its full potential. His proposal at the London AGM that CAMRA should become the Campaign for Real Ale was, like all truly great ideas, breathtakingly simple: it at once preserved the name CAMRA and told the public what we were all about in a few words.

It was to prove the turning point of the Campaign, so much so that brewers who at first were incensed by any suggestion that they were producing *un*real ale began to use the very phrase themselves once they had seen the light. Now, even dictionaries recognise the term.

We *have* come a long way, haven't we?

Michael Hardman

Footnote...

One CAMRA myth that needs to be laid to rest involves the question of which was the Campaign's first Branch. A plaque on the outside of the Farrier's Arms in St Albans claims that the first CAMRA Branch meeting was held there. It was not. The first Branch of the Campaign had been launched in West Yorkshire some months earlier and was thriving until its founder, John Brearley, died in an accident in Munich towards the end of 1972. The efforts of these Yorkshire pioneers and the memory of John deserve better recognition.

CAMRA: THE HISTORY

THERE ARE TWO types of history: the events, recounted factually and chronologically, one by one; and the interpretation, the attempt to extrapolate those wider trends or longer-term outcomes which give the events significance. This short history of CAMRA will provide the first, as uncontentiously as is possible in a movement which has, from time to time, been torn by internal debates reminiscent of medieval schisms, and then a more personal view of the second.

The story, plain and simple

The idea of a campaign to revitalise British ale arose when four friends from the north-west of England found themselves bemoaning the state of British beer and pubs during a holiday in Ireland in 1971.

Elsewhere in this book, Michael Hardman, one of the four, gives more of the background in a personal reminiscence.

The remarkable point about CAMRA is not the idea, for it was not entirely original: the 1960s had seen various groups concerned with beer, notably the Society for the Preservation of Beers from the Wood (SPBW). It was that it caught on: first, it did not meet the fate of all those other plans to change the world hatched every day in Irish bars, which disappear with the froth on the next pint of stout; and second, it chimed with the mood of the times in the early 1970s, after a decade when pubs and their beers had been blitzed as a result of the multiplicity of mergers which had created six dominant companies in British brewing (Allied, Bass, Courage, Scottish & Newcastle, Watney and Whitbread) and the trend towards a few heavily-advertised national brands of keg beer (Double Diamond, Worthington E, Tavern, Tartan, Red Barrel, and Tankard). At last, beer drinkers were in a frame of mind to react in a positive and aggressive campaign.

Nonetheless, CAMRA's take-off was gradual at first. Graham Lees, one of the founding four, took on the organisational role. In a natural development for a campaign launched by three journalists, a newsletter was launched, titled *What's Brewing;* its first issue was a one-page A4 mini-tabloid. And one brewery re-opened: as recounted elsewhere in this book, Martin Sykes pioneered the way for many later micro-brewery operators by taking the bold step of recommencing brewing at Selby.

By October 1973, CAMRA had 5000 members. Three seminal publications, and the wider publicity they generated, attracted more and more people to join. First was Frank Baillie's *The Beer-Drinker's Companion,* cataloguing and evaluating beers and breweries. Second was Chris Hutt's *The Death of the English Pub,* a sustained polemic against the brewers' vandalism of their tied houses. And third was Richard Boston's entertaining weekly column on all aspects of beer in *The Guardian,* a series later collected in his book *Beer and Skittles* (1976).

When in November 1973 CAMRA ran its first major demonstration, a march to protest against the closure of Joules Brewery (founded in the 12th century), over 600 members gathered in the quiet town of Stone, Staffordshire, and the event gained wide press and TV coverage.

By February 1974, there were 9000 members, and in a development of great significance for the future style and operation of CAMRA as an organisation, the first local Branches had been formed as voluntary associations of activists in a particular area.

1974 was remarkable also for the development of three key campaigning weapons. The first book-style *Good Beer Guide* was produced – and swiftly withdrawn, for lawyers for the distributors, Waddingtons, objected to the entry for Watney's brewery ("Avoid like the plague") as too risky. With the new text "Avoid at all costs", the presses rolled, and 30,000 copies were sold in 7 months. Elsewhere in this book, Jill Adam chronicles the progress of the *GBG* to its current position as the UK's best-selling guide to beer and pubs.

The two other campaigning weapons provided a demonstration of direct consumer power which the brewers could not afford to ignore. The first Beer Festival, in the Corn Exchange, Cambridge, in July 1974, sold half its supply of some 70 firkins (9 gallon casks) in the first day. Sales more than doubled in each of the next three years. The beer festival idea caught on, as John Bishopp explains in his article on the first national beer festival at Covent Garden, the precursor for the Great British Beer Festivals of later years.

And finally CAMRA bought its first pubs, via a separate company. (CAMRA was not at this time legally incorporated, so could not easily own property.) The motive for establishing CAMRA (Real Ale) Investments Ltd. was essentially defeatist, or at least defensive: in 1974, most members of the campaign in their sober moments expected to lose in the long run, and to be faced (by 1980 or so) with keg beer in virtually all pubs. If real ale survived, the expectation was that it would do so as a tiny minority taste, and one way of ensuring at least this degree of survival was to set up a pub-owning chain, which might eventually acquire a brewery, and so guarantee continued supplies of cask beer at selected pubs around the country. But immediately on opening, the first two pubs (The White Gates at Hyde and The Old Fox in Bristol) were phenomenally successful. They and the other CAMRAIL pubs provided a clear model for free houses serving a wide range of well-kept real ales, a formula copied so extensively that CAMRAIL eventually became the victim of its own success by removing any real reason for its existence: when pubs everywhere sold real ale again, there was little need for CAMRA to own and run a handful of free houses.

By 1976, CAMRA had nearly 30,000 members; actually, the HQ administration and records were in such poor order at this time that no-one really knows how many members there were.

The breweries were beginning to get the real ale message, and handpumps serving cask-conditioned beer were being exhumed from pub cellars and re-installed on bar tops. The first national beer festival, at Covent Garden in September 1975, prompted a wave of new beer launches from Newcastle to Cornwall. In June 1976, a major breakthrough happened when Ind Coope launched Burton Ale into 1000 pubs simultaneously. The tide was on the turn, and CAMRA was acclaimed by the then Michael Young (now Lord Young of Dartington), President of the Consumers' Association, as "the most successful consumer movement in Europe".

1976 was noteworthy for four other developments. First, CAMRA became a company limited by guarantee. This safeguarded both the unpaid volunteer members of the National Executive and the staff such as the Editor of *What's Brewing*, who would have been individually liable if CAMRA had been sued for defamation or simply gone bankrupt. Second, because of a misguided decision to peg the membership subscription at £2 for two years at a time of great activity and high inflation, the campaign ran into the first of a series of financial problems that were to occupy the time and efforts of many leading members until the mid-1980s. In the first major blow for better information about beer, the *GBG* listed the original gravities of many beers; Chris Bruton explains the background to this in a detailed article. And finally, in its first real effort at influencing legislation, CAMRA supported a Private Member's Bill to extend pub opening hours which had been introduced by Kenneth Clarke (now, 1992, Home Secretary) but which was talked out by opponents in the Commons.

The next year, 1977, saw the real ale revolution in full flow, with significant developments such as Bass promoting real ale in over a thousand of its pubs in the north-west of England, and real ale being introduced to 52 Trust House Forte outlets. Detailed technical work began to show results too, with the report of the Food Standards Committee on ingredients listing (only now, and via the European Commission, nearing implementation), and the major report on beer prices from the Price Commission condemning the Big Six, exactly as CAMRA had argued, for their monopolistic practices at the customer's expense.

More ominously, 1977 saw CAMRA riven by internal dissension as a result of the introduction in May of a beer called Truman's Tap into some 100 pubs. It was not the beer, but the method of its dispense by air pressure without venting, which was the point of contention: arguably the dispense method offended against CAMRA's view that no CO_2 gas should be used to serve a beer or to cover it with a "blanket" to preserve it from deterioration (and flavour maturation) by contact with the atmosphere.

And the front page of July's *What's Brewing* featured a new enemy for the campaign: lager. It is now difficult to recall precisely how appalling the early British-brewed lagers were: fake in virtually every aspect, they had almost no redeeming feature except their icy coldness on a hot day. But the mid-1970s saw the brewers' first moves to switch from dying keg bitter to the new style of light, fizzy pseudo-continental keg lager.

1978 was chiefly remarkable for a "voluntary" arrangement among the big brewers to swap large numbers of pubs in different parts of the country to dilute their local monopolies without ceding control over their total share of the beer market. Instigated by the then Secretary of State for Prices and Consumer Protection, Roy Hattersley, as a consequence of the 1976 Price Commission report, the plan was implemented dilatorily and patchily and died with the fall of the Labour Government in 1979.

Through 1978 and 1979, the swing back to cask beer continued unabated. In May 1978, Ansells put real ale back into 250 pubs, and in April 1979, arch-enemy Watneys introduced Norwich Castle Bitter into 500 pubs, albeit in kegs, not proper casks, and with an adapted keg dispenser to allow spiling and venting.

The symbolic culmination of this phase of CAMRA's existence came in June 1979, when Watney's killed off their flagship keg beer brand, Watney's Red, the epitome of everything that had gone wrong with British beer and its marketing. It seemed the campaign was won.

The brewers would have liked nothing better for us to believe that this was indeed the case. And a key problem in the early 1980s was to convince even CAMRA members that the campaign did have a role and a future, especially when internal dissension and financial strains were at their height in the early 1980s. The problem was that the campaign had been *too* successful: it was easy for the brewery PR people to suggest that CAMRA had done its job, that its members could now retire to some snug public bar, and that cask beer would be secure for evermore – with the brewers. CAMRA membership declined – at one point to below 15,000; some financial turkeys came home to roost; and generally the campaign suffered from burnout, with longstanding volunteer activists deciding their exhausting efforts deserved a break, the central HQ adminstration close to breakdown, and the media bored with stories about beer.

The 1980s started badly for CAMRA in many ways. In 1980, another Bill to liberalise Britain's antiquated licensing hours was lost. Beer broke through the 50p a pint price barrier, and raced away towards the £1 pint. CAMRA's attempt to reach a wider audience through publishing a magazine about beer, on public sale through newsagents, had to be discontinued because the campaign's finances could not stand the losses for long enough to judge properly whether the venture might have been successful. Alexandra Palace, venue for the Great British Beer Festival, was burnt out in a mighty conflagration only a few weeks before the Festival was due to take place, and only heroic efforts by the volunteer team kept the event afloat (an appropriate word as the rain came down on the two huge marquees provided as an alternative venue by Haringey Council). Finally, a year of problems was ended with the sudden and tragic death from asthma of the campaign's Chairman, Joe Goodwin, a larger-than-life figure who had tirelessly devoted himself to the cause.

1981 was a pivotal year for CAMRA as amid all its present and pressing problems, policy and financial strategies were hammered out that began to lay the foundations for future recovery. The AGM saw a horrendous financial report, with a loss on the year of over £47,000, and as a result carried a package of near-emergency financial measures which I had originated: chief among them were a 40% increase in membership subscription, from £5 to £7, and a levy of 10% on the surpluses generated by Branches. The expectation that Branches would help to finance the campaign's activities has today translated into voluntary donations which are one of the central organisation's main sources of income.

The same AGM saw a key policy debate which was to shape attitudes for the future. Posing crudely the choices ahead for CAMRA, a motion was carried which demanded that the campaign should go "back to basics" and concentrate on increasing the proportion of real ale brewed and its availability. "Diversifications" – into licensing hours, or monopolies, or the European arena – were thereby meant to be ruled out. The motion was mistimed and backward-looking, especially in a year when (according to CAMRA's own estimate) more than half of the pubs in Britain sold real ale again for the first time since 1970. The National Executive, not for the first time selectively ignoring policy set by the AGM, gradually put forward wider policy motions to the AGM during the early 1980s and succeeded in broadening the campaign's sphere of interest and scope for action, until in 1988, when another narrowly fundamentalist motion calling for all diversifications to be abandoned immediately was put before the AGM, it was heavily defeated. To most involved, the way forward seemed not to be an attempt to repeat former successes, or merely to continue with campaigning themes and objectives which even our own members had begun to tire of, but to move the campaign on to new ground where fresh victories might be won. An early sign of this was the publication in 1981 of the campaign's policy document *Whose Pint Is It Anyway?* Though the politics of this publication look strange with the hindsight of the 1990s, it was CAMRA's first major attempt to produce mature thinking on tackling the monopoly power of the major brewers.

Finally, in this pivotal year of 1981, new Company Secretary Iain Dobson made a much-needed start on overhauling the HQ administration and, in particular, the financial and membership systems. One instance of the problems will suffice. CAMRA had previously implemented a scheme for members to pay subscriptions by standing order from their bank accounts. But no provision had been made to identify the members from whom the payments came. Consequently, non-payers continued to receive *What's Brewing*, and when in 1981 the subscription rate was increased from £5 to £7, those who did not increase their standing orders could not be identified. The membership list was maintained on a manual metal plate address system, which was slow and cumbersome. The solutions, which involved major expenditure computerising the membership system at a time of great financial strain, plus phasing out the standing order method of payment and phasing in direct debit, required considerable courage, expertise and patience to stick with a long-term strategy. Even today, in 1992, out of the thousands of standing order payers who have been identified, there are still 25 who send CAMRA £4 a year from their bank accounts – and receive absolutely nothing in return.

The early 1980s were a time of relative prosperity, when buoyant personal disposable incomes meant that the fall in beer production slowed and the pressure on the industry for efficiency through closure of idle plant was not so acute. Brewery closures and takeovers, seen historically, were at a low ebb, so that CAMRA had time to sort out its internal problems without the same level of frantic external action as was the norm in the 1970s and later 1980s. Even so, there were some portents of what was to come in the early 1980s.

In the first intervention by the EEC – as it then was – in the British brewing industry, the Commission outlined proposals to end vertical integration and the tied house system because of the anti-competitive nature of the structure of the industry. Even though these moves came to nothing at the time, there could have been no clearer indication that "back to basics" was not an option: the world had moved on.

In the following year, 1982, the then Home Office Minister Tim Raison MP conceded that public opinion had swung in favour of more liberal licensing hours. It was, of course, to be some years before the politicians took any notice of this development, and nearly two years before the trade itself, with CAMRA involvement, set up a lobby and campaigning group (FLAG – the Flexible Licensing Hours Action Group) to push at the opening doors of the House of Commons.

1983 saw the first sign of renewed contraction in the brewing industry as Wolverhampton & Dudley bid for Davenport's. Great effort was expended by CAMRA in opposing brewery takeovers for the simple reason that, almost without exception, takeover led to the closure of the victim brewery and the eventual discontinuation of the beers it had brewed. But equally almost without exception, CAMRA's efforts were unsuccessful in the longer term; a predator thwarted on its first attempt would almost always return successfully on a later occasion to finish off its prey, or the victim, weakened by the struggle, would succumb to some form of defensive merger or another predator. The instances of the two companies bid for by the expansionist Scottish and Newcastle Breweries are typical: though the S&N bid for Cameron's of Hartlepool in May 1984 was defeated, it led to Cameron's long and unhappy subjugation to other owners; and Matthew Brown of Blackburn, who survived S&N's first bid attempt in May 1985, lost out to the tartan terror in the long run.

In almost a scene-setting exercise for 1985-6, Watney's axed their Norwich brewery and merged Websters and Wilsons in what can be seen now as the first step on their strategic exit from brewing.

It was as well that CAMRA had made excellent progress with its internal re-organisation (membership bottomed out at under 15,000 and then began to increase, and the strict financial measures resulted in a £17,000 surplus), for the events of late 1985 proved just how much work there was still for the campaign to do. The pace of takeovers and closures accelerated, as Mansfield swallowed Hull, Marston's took over Border, Mitchell's snatched near neighbour Yates and Jackson, Boddington's grabbed Higsons, and Greenall Whitley marched into Simpkiss and in a symbolic gesture of pure insult poured the final brew down the drain as they closed the brewery.

CAMRA's protests led the Office of Fair Trading to refer the situation in the industry, and specifically the issue of vertical integration, to the Monopolies and Mergers Commission for investigation on the prima facie grounds of a monopolistic structure appearing to work against the interests of competition and the consumer. Elsewhere in this book, Steve Cox has outlined the progress and outcome of the M&MC's deliberations.

The mere fact of an investigation did not deter brewers from takeovers. 1986 saw closures of subsidiaries, with Vaux closing Darley's and Lorimer's and Matthew Brown closing Carlisle, and "agreed" takeovers of Home Brewery by Scottish and Newcastle and of one of the most famous names from the early days of the real ale revival – Ruddle's – by Watney's.

These were the first signs of major changes in the brewing industry: over the five years since 1987, the impact of the M&MC proposals, combined with the onset of a long-lasting recession which has led to falling beer consumption overall and increasing intervention in the UK sector of major international players, has altered the structure and character of the beer and pubs business in the UK.

The first sign of overseas interest emerged in October 1986, when the Australian conglomerate Elders IXL bought Courage and John Smiths from Hanson Trust, which had taken over the Imperial Group and "unbundled" it by selling major component businesses. Elders planned to establish a major presence in the European market, an intention confirmed by its bid in November 1988 for Scottish & Newcastle. But, like many other rapidly-expanding multinationals, Elders was taken by surprise by the speed and severity of the onset of the recession and the decline in its stock valuation, especially after "Black Monday" in October 1987, and was forced into savage retrenchment by its bankers. But overseas interest in the British industry is here to stay: Allied merged with Carlsberg of Denmark in November 1991, and early in 1992 Grolsch of Holland bought Ruddles. In response, CAMRA has become increasingly international in its outlook, and took the lead in forming the European Beer Consumers' Union with other national pressure groups.

Contraction in the industry continued over the years 1987-1992, with the brewers tending to blame "the M&MC" for many of the later closures. The real reason was the recession, which forced many companies to strip out surplus capacity, close idle plant, lay off staff, realise assets and cut costs, compounded by increases in the price of beer which outstripped inflation and had the effect of further depressing consumption. Brewers were caught in a vicious downward spiral partly of their own making.

With six to ten breweries under threat of closure each year from 1987 onwards, there was much for CAMRA to campaign about. In 1987, Watney's closed Norwich and Drybrough's. Greene King closed Rayments. Greenall Whitley closed Wem. Whitbread closed Chester's and Wethered's of Marlow. And Scottish & Newcastle launched their second bid for Matthew Brown, which was quickly successful. The only bright spot was that after many months of uncertainty following a family rift, Bateman's of Wainfleet was kept open by the heroic efforts of George Bateman in raising the cash to buy out those family members who wanted to sell up. All of these events brought CAMRA much media attention, and the public began to realise that there was a reason for having a consumer group to fight for choice. As a result, membership began to rise rapidly.

CAMRA was not idle on other issues. First, in January 1987, backbencher Allan Stewart MP introduced a Private Member's Bill to liberalise English licensing hours. Though the Bill fell with the General Election, it had demonstrated that the measure had achieved popular support, and (perhaps more importantly) it attracted little more than token opposition from the "alcohol abuse" lobby. Before the end of the year, a Government Bill to introduce flexible licensing hours was on its way through the Houses of Parliament, becoming law in summer 1988. So one of the longest-lasting temporary pieces of legislation (the Defence of the Realm Act 1916) was finally amended, and the people of England were once more allowed to drink in pubs in the afternoons legally.

CAMRA was also thrashing out its policy on the issue of the tied house system. After some internal debate, it was accepted that the preservation of the leading small and medium sized independent brewers required the continuance of a limited tie, to give such brewers a guaranteed and protected market; but equally that the major brewers' sheer number of tied houses constituted a distortion of the market and was fundamentally anti-competitive. In January 1988, this view was substantially endorsed by the M&MC itself, when in its "letter" or interim report it stated that it was persuaded that a "complex monopoly" situation did in fact exist in the beer industry. The final M&MC report, published in May 1989, vindicated CAMRA's claims, and though it was immediately and strongly attacked by the brewers, who in the main have spent the last 4 years inventing ways of avoiding or circumventing the M&MC final conclusions, it has led to much greater freedom of trade in beer in pubs. A particularly welcome provision was the ruling that the "guest beer" which every tied house tenant should be free to take should be a real ale. This was a direct outcome of CAMRA's campaigning.

An indication that far-reaching changes in the industry were imminent came even before the M&MC's final report, when in August 1988 Elders IXL announced plans to separate into two by floating off its pubs as a kind of arm's-length company. This was the precursor of even more revolutionary developments as the M&MC's attempt to demolish the high degree of vertical integration in the brewing industry (with the main beer producers also owning the bulk of the retail outlets and so able to stifle competition) forced companies to consider a choice between being brewers or being pub owners. In the shake-out, Greenall Whitley decided in September 1990 to quit brewing and close its Warrington and Nottingham (Shipstone's) breweries, following a similar move a year earlier by another leading regional brewer, Boddington's, which in a betrayal of its proud history sold out in November 1989 to Whitbread. But the biggest such move happened in March 1990, when Grand Metropolitan announced that it would swap its breweries for 5,000 Courage and John Smith's pubs owned by Elders IXL. If the axing of Watney's Red in 1979 was the symbolic culmination of the 1970s and the first phase of CAMRA's history, then the symbolic culmination of the 1980s and CAMRA's impact on the big brewers was the decision by Watney's to stop brewing altogether.

As the 1980s ended, CAMRA was in far better shape than anyone would have predicted in 1980. So complete was the turn-round in the Campaign's finances that in May 1989 it was able to buy its HQ building in St Albans, 34 Alma Road, and to pay off the bank loan within two years. Membership continued to soar, with the 30,000th member being signed up in September 1991. After a key motion to the 1988 National Conference calling for a long-term strategy to be developed, the Campaign has a forward plan which is regularly revised to take account of developing circumstances. Both the HQ administration and the "volunteer" side of the movement have been run with increasing professionalism through the 1980s, with the necessary managerial approach not over-riding the voluntary nature of the Campaign. The cask ale section of the market is continuing to grow, and new small breweries are still being opened despite the recession. But there is still plenty for CAMRA to do in the 1990s.

The interpretation

The history of CAMRA falls into three phases, roughly coterminous with the three decades of the 1970s, 1980s, and 1990s.

In the 1970s, the priority was on urgent and immediate action. The threat to the survival of real ale was clear and simple. The need to campaign by all possible means to preserve cask beer was paramount. Other issues were not only seen as being of less importance, but could never inspire such passion and dedication as was evident in the mid-1970s. CAMRA was, in effect, a single-issue pressure group. Where its policy on other issues was considered, decisions tended to be ad hoc, liable to reversal, and not necessarily consistent with one another.

At the end of the 1970s, CAMRA was the victim of its own success. It had, apparently, conclusively won the single-issue battle it had chosen to fight, for the survival and increased availability of real ale. Having won, it had, in the eyes of many commentators, left itself with nothing to do and no further reason for existing.

This was actually a presentational error by the Campaign itself, for its Memorandum of Association, drafted in 1976, outlined very broad aims, far wider than the single issue of real ale.

The presentational error was compounded by an internal battle over CAMRA's future direction, with many activists objecting to attempts to broaden the Campaign's remit into other issues as a "diversification" from its real purpose, and calling for a return to campaigning for real ale and handpumps on bars in a "back to basics" motion to the AGM.

The 1980s saw CAMRA redefine its role, internally and publicly, and forge a financially-secure, professional and well-managed consumer lobbying operation to carry out the role. As a result of a more strategic approach to policy and key issues, in a series of cumulative steps (such as the codification of policy in the Policy File, the establishment of a Strategy Group, and the presentation of key policy motions to the AGM by the NE), the Campaign began to review its policy, determine its aims in relation to the brewing industry, and think long-term not just about the survival of cask ale but about all the factors, from customer preferences through to pub design, which affected the future of real beer.

Consequently, when towards the end of the 1980s issues such as the anti-competitiveness of the tied house system and the high degree of vertical integration in the brewing industry began to gain prominence, the Campaign was in good shape to tackle them.

But there was a cost. A noticeable divide opened up between the 200 or so people leading the Campaign who were up-to-date on developments, understood the issues, and were part of the central mechanism for considering policy choices, and the rest of the membership. The "thinktanking" which defined CAMRA's new approach necessarily went on in small groups, and took a considerable while to percolate through the communications channels to the "grass-roots" members. Internal gripes about the National Executive being "out of touch" were rife in the mid-1980s.

The 1990s will see a further evolution in CAMRA's role. The decade looks likely to see increasing globalisation of markets: witness Grand Metropolitan's major involvement in North America, and the increasing availability of beers from Canada and Mexico in the UK. British brewing cannot afford to be insular if it is not to go the way of our camera and micro-chip makers. In turn, this means that a consumer organisation needs to be able to track trends and developments globally but respond locally.

International trends are not wholly against CAMRA, despite the uniqueness of British real ale. Recessionary pressures are forcing consumers to consider value for money in choosing drinks, and this, together with increased publicity about the health dangers of alcohol, is leading to a tendency for "drinking less but better" and a swing to premium products, especially real ales and genuine European beers rather than UK-brewed imitations. And the ethos of the 1990s (while it has not yet developed the full fin-de-siecle ripe, dark and decadent naughtiness of the 1890s) has swung against the superficial "greed is good" me-tooism of the 1980s boom years, towards a concern with intrinsic values and non-material issues. Rich dark beers like porters are enjoying a renaissance among people who six years ago would have drunk champagne.

Against this background, CAMRA's role as both watchdog on the international brewing industry, and consumer think-tank for how that industry can best develop in touch with its customers, seems secure both in terms of approach and application.

Tony Millns

ILLUSTRATIONS

1. Bill Tidy's view of the importance of CAMRA on its 21st birthday...

2. The early days – a CAMRA demo against the closure of Joule's

3. CAMRA Chairman Chris Bruton leads a protest in 1977 against Courage's policy of keg beer only in London

4. The four founders of CAMRA celebrating the 10th birthday (left to right, Jim Makin, Bill Mellor, Michael Hardman, Graham Lees)

5. David Bellamy, conserving a pint, opens the 1979 Great British Beer Festival with (right) CAMRA Chairman Joe Goodwin

6. Miles Templeman of Whitbread enters the lion's den of the 1991 CAMRA National Conference in Sheffield

7. Roy Hattersley (then Secretary of State for Prices and Consumer Protection) opening the 1978 Great British Beer Festival

8. The tasting panel for the 1987 Champion Beer of Britain taking its task seriously, with Madame Rose Blancquaert of the Liefmans Brewery and Michael Jackson on the left

9. Sexist signature: Bill Tidy opens the 1980 Great British Beer Festival by autographing a lady

10. After Alexandra Palace was destroyed by fire in 1980, the Great British Beer Festival took place in two huge marquees...

11. ...while 1991's Festival happened in the no less unlikely surroundings of the London Arena in Docklands

12. The front page of the first issue of *What's Brewing*

2

3

4

5

6

7

8

9

10

11

Journal of CAMRA, the Campaign for the Revitalisation of Ale   JUNE 1972

Voice of the drinking man...

WELCOME to the first issue of the Campaign for the Revitalisation of Ale's own monthly journal, which will keep members fully informed of progress in the fight to improve Britain's beer. It is hoped you will all help to make What's Brewing a lively newspaper by sending in your own news and views.

TOP PUB IS FORCED TO STOP 'FRAUD'

CAMRA has won its first battle against the flashy gimmicks that disguise bad ale.

The battle began when a number of members reported that Draught Bass being sold at Dirty Dick's - one of London's best-known pubs - was pressurised, even though it was apparently being served straight from huge wooden barrels behind the bar.

Two CAMRA officials went along to the pub and heard more than a dozen customers asking for "Draught Bass from the wood". But on tasting the beer, the CAMRA men found it gassy and sweet.

They tackled a barman about the barrels. At first, he insisted that they were genuine, but later admitted that pipes led from the taps, through the hollow barrels and into the cellar where they were connected to a press-urised cask.

CAMRA's Complaints Committee reported the "fraud" to the City of London Weights and Measures Department, asking for prosecution under the Trade Descriptions Act. Inspectors from the Department visited the pub and complained to Finch's, the wine and spirit merchants who own Dirty Dick's.

The company agreed to avoid prosecution by displaying notices pointing out that the ale was pressurised.

Mr R.J. Hearn, a director of Finch's, told What's Brewing: "We were at fault, and I am very grateful to CAMRA for pointing this out. We don't want our products to be misrepresented."

The CAMRA Complaints Committee is now considering similar action against pubs owned by other firms.

CAMRA officials in brewing study

TEAMS of CAMRA officials are this month inspecting two London breweries as part of a series of fact-finding missions.

The teams will be paying special attention to the difference in pro- est bitter, according to the Sunday Mirror, and Guinness's Park Royal brewery.

CAMRA General Secretary Graham Lees said: "This type of investigation is vital if we are to speak with an

STOP PRESS

A TEAM of area organisers has been appointed to increase CAMRA's

SELBY BREWERY

MY GRANDFATHER, LIONEL Sykes, used to be partial to a pint of beer from Middlebrough's Brewery at Selby, which is why he decided to buy the business when it came up for sale in 1944. It had never been a particularly successful brewery, and had struggled to survive the difficulties of the war years, but Lionel kept it going at a time when many small breweries were falling victim to takeover and closure. Sadly he died in 1952, and the family decided to stop brewing and concentrate instead on Guinness bottling. A deal was struck with Duttons Brewery of Blackburn to supply them with Guinness, and in return to buy their draught beer. This arrangement kept the business going until Duttons were taken over by Whitbreads in the 1960s. Eventually our three tied pubs were sold and the brewery survived for a few more years on the sale of bottled Guinness to a handful of clubs in the pit villages of South Yorkshire.

I came to Selby by chance in 1968, fresh from University, to begin a job teaching law at Hull College of Commerce. I had nowhere to live, but persuaded my uncle to let me use the empty brewer's flat above the brewery office until I found somewhere to live in Hull. I am still living there 24 years later.

Soon after my arrival my uncle decided to retire and dispose of the business. As I'd done nothing about looking for another place to live, I persuaded him to let me help run the brewery for a while. The prospect of spending weekends and college holidays travelling round all the local pubs looking for business certainly had its attractions, and it wasn't long before I began to do it full time. Out of loyalty to our product I started to drink bottled Guinness and soon got to like it. It seemed infinitely better than the cold, fizzy keg beers on sale in most of the places I called at on my rounds.

Gradually I realised that the brewery couldn't survive for ever on its sales of bottled Guinness. We needed other strings to our bow, and I began to dream about resuming brewing, especially after I'd had a pint or two. After all, I thought, the brewhouse was still there, even though most of the equipment was too dilapidated to use, and we had a regular set of customers for the Guinness. Surely it ought to be possible to persuade some of them to try a new draught beer?

But there were problems too. I didn't know anything at all about the technical side of brewing, or where to get supplies of malt, hops, yeast and so on. Our funds were limited, and there didn't seem to be any suppliers of small scale cheap brewing equipment. The whole industry seemed to be geared up to modern hi-tech production methods. Another stumbling block would be getting the necessary approval from Customs and Excise.

Reluctantly I decided to let the revival of Selby Ales remain as a pipe dream for the future, and opted instead for a deal to distribute Theakston's cask beers in East Yorkshire.

Then in 1970 two unexpected things happened. One day out of the blue a letter arrived from a stranger, Basil Savage, a brewer at John Smith's in nearby Tadcaster, suggesting that we might like to resume brewing at Selby and offering his services. Shortly afterwards, in the course of a weekend trip to the Midlands I learnt that two home-brew pubs – The Druid's Head at Coseley and The Britannia at Loughborough – had recently closed and their equipment was up for sale. Suddenly we were in business!

Within a year we had refurbished the brewhouse, obtained a supply of wooden casks, and were ready to begin test brewing. We opted at first for a high strength bitter brewed just from malt, hops, yeast, and water. As well as being more wholesome this would also be simpler to produce. The first brew to be sold was mashed on 25th November 1972 and went out just in time for Christmas. It was greeted enthusiastically, and received national publicity in the media.

Initial sales were much better than we had hoped, but to our surprise little interest was shown by our existing customers. Instead, unexpectedly, we gained a large number of new customers – student bars, draught beer shops, beer festivals, real ale pubs, beer agencies and so on, as far away as London, Edinburgh, Newcastle Manchester and Nottingham. Our great good fortune was to have begun brewing at about the same time as CAMRA was born. A few years earlier we would probably have failed completely.

Although it was flattering to have so much interest shown in Selby Ales from far and wide, we realised that we would never get rich by delivering odd barrels all over the place. What we really needed was regular local trade. My ultimate ambition was to build up a traditional small brewery supplying a few pubs of our own. Fortunately in 1973 we were able to buy and re-open the Board Inn at Howden, a derelict ex-John Smith's pub about ten miles from Selby. This was followed a few years later by the Brewery Tap in Selby, an off-licence specialising in take-home draught beer.

In recent years we have consolidated rather than expanded. This enables us to concentrate on quality and keep prices down. The business is healthier financially than it has ever been.

There are hundreds of small breweries now. People sometimes ask me if I am jealous of the competition. No – I take it as a compliment!

Martin Sykes

THE COVENT GARDEN BEER FESTIVAL

"COVENT GARDEN" was the beer festival that had to happen, but in the event, nearly didn't.

When, in November 1973, the late Peter Pearce suggested that the Cambridge Branch of CAMRA should organise a four-day beer festival, aimed at introducing the general public to the wide variety of taste and character associated with the real ales still available, rather than the more usual one-day "thrash" mostly patronised by the CAMRA faithful, the Campaign had taken an irrevocable step on the path which inevitably led to Covent Garden and the national beer festivals which followed.

So it was that, in early 1975, Eric Spragett, Chris Bruton and I were asked to look at the feasibility of mounting such an event in London, providing as wide a selection of beers as possible but stopping short of a truly national festival.

At first everything went smoothly. Three venues were considered: Camden Lock, Alexandra Palace and St. Katherine's Dock. The latter was our unanimous choice. Planning reached an advanced stage – the lease had been agreed, breweries approached, and even the provision of boats and lifeguards, to rescue the more enthusiastic punters, had been arranged – when the Fire Officer stepped in and, effectively, ruled out the use of the site.

Thus, in May 1975, we had nearly all the organisational structure for a large festival in place, but no venue! It was at this juncture that urgent talks took place with the GLC to find a suitable site, in time for a major beer festival planned for September! Luckily, the Covent Garden Community Association were actively engaged in revitalising the old market area and, with their invaluable help, the GLC were persuaded to let us use the historic but then disused and somewhat derelict Flower Market. To paraphrase Eric's marvellous slogan, Covent Garden would be alive with real ale.

The problems were immense. Every possible contact was tapped and browbeaten into supplying expertise, labour and hardware to build new toilets, to replace much of the old wiring, to install new lighting... The list of things to do seemed endless.

The stalwart cellarmen – Mike Nutt and myself – had a slightly easier passage; the good relationships and mutual respect already built up through numerous local festivals bore fruit. Over 30 breweries, from Wales, Scotland and from all over England, agreed to supply more than 50 different real ales; a mouth-watering array of beers all, for the first time, under one roof. Indeed, such was the enthusiasm of the breweries that not only did regional rivals co-operate and share transport to get their ale to London but one micro-brewery, Pollards of Reddish, was virtually launched at the event.

Neither was the stillage a problem. The old flower stalls might well have been designed for beer barrels; the top shelf could take three kilderkins and the drop-flap another three. However, what we hadn't appreciated, until virtually the last minute, was that this excellent stillage didn't come complete with bar counters – so we didn't use any and put the clock back to the time when beer was drawn straight from the barrel, stillaged in a corner of the pub's tap room.

One last major problem was the licence. A week before the event we didn't have one! Rumours were rife that our application was going to be opposed but, in the event, with Chiswick brewers Fuller, Smith and Turner agreeing to become our licensee, the application was granted without difficulty.

By some miracle, engineered by Eric, the festival's superb general factotum, all building work was successfully completed and, as the first beer deliveries were being made, the mammoth task of sweeping out the whole building was also finished not a moment too soon, as the whole area was then cordoned off due to the discovery of a suspected bomb. The offending article was a briefcase, with a festival sticker firmly attached. I still have the briefcase!

This was an inauspicious start to our relationship with Bow Street's Police Station. However, as the festival progressed their enthusiasm blossomed. No thanks are enough for the way in which they looked after us, especially when the queues became too large for us to handle (over a quarter of a mile long on the Friday night). We didn't even mind off-duty officers using their warrant cards to dodge the queues and gain admittance through a back door.

By the morning of Tuesday, 9th September 1975 we had all the beer on stillage and enough, or so we thought, tapped and spiled for the first two days of the festival. Then, at 11.00am, following a press review and a tour of the bars by Illtyd Harrington (the then deputy leader of the GLC), Chris Holmes (the CAMRA Chairman) opened the doors of the biggest pub in the UK, and all hell broke loose!

To me, it seemed like the first Cambridge festival all over again, albeit on a much larger scale. Hundreds of people quickly overwhelmed the front-of-house staff selling beer tokens (no monies were taken at the bars) and the commemorative beer glasses. Our bar staff were soon stretched to the limit.

Although Denis Palmer had arranged for over 200 CAMRA members to work at the event, this was immediately found to be inadequate. Many members, who had come as customers, found themselves press-ganged into service; not a few stayed and worked until the end on the Saturday. It is impossible to pay too high a tribute to our staff, all of whom gave freely of their time, for without their cheerful (?) willingness to work a 14-hour day, we would never have achieved the success that we did.

Anthony Gibson's pre-festival publicity had paid off only too well. The simple message of good beer, brewed and served traditionally, accompanied by wholesome food, had caught the imagination of the media and the public at large. Never before, or since, has the Campaign and the idea of real ale had such a high and favourable world-wide exposure.

The first two days had everything: crowds which surpassed our wildest hopes (over 40,000 by the end of the festival), the Pollards bar being drunk dry by the end of the first session, and the other beers disappearing at an alarming rate, a robbery, new members from all over the world signing on in their droves (over 800 by the Saturday – many of whom immediately volunteered for bar work), Christian Muteau, on the CAMRA stall, everlastingly complaining about running out of stock, and the 15,000 commemorative glasses being sold out by the Wednesday evening.

We needed, therefore, to take urgent steps if the festival was to stay open until Saturday 13th. Fuller's solved one problem by supplying, at an hour's notice, thousands of plastic glasses. Emergency beer deliveries were also desperately required.

It was here that the already accepted success of the festival came to our aid. With many brewery directors and head brewers actually present, it was relatively easy to make the arrangements. So many breweries turned up trumps. Particular mention must be made of Belhaven of Dunbar and Brains of Cardiff. The latter, for the first time in their history, arranged for a brewery dray to leave Wales and cross the Severn Bridge into England! Belhaven loaded a van with as much ale as it could take, told the drivers to get to London as soon as possible and then to take a couple of days off and enjoy the festival.

Thanks to these and numerous other friends, enough beer was delivered to keep our customers happy for the last three hectic days. In all, over 150,000 pints were supped.

Stock levels were never the problem at the food counters: deliveries of countless numbers of whole Stilton, Cheddar and Red Windsor (the festival favourite) cheeses, as well as van-loads of bread, became a regular early-morning sight. The difficulty was for Gill Knight and her excellent team to keep up with the ravenous demands of our public, but cope they did and quite superbly. Nobody went hungry, especially the staff. Asked, some weeks later, for her comments, a still bemused Gill Knight could only demand a CAMRA policy on the supply of pickles at beer festivals!

Somehow, we managed to meet nearly all the demands and didn't close until the advertised time on the Saturday night – no mean achievement. The only quiet time I remember was at midnight, when all the staff had gone for their last trains and a couple of us walked the bars, checking and preparing the beer for the next day.

It was a great event, but there was no escaping the relief when it was all over. The party was mind-blowing! Certainly we learnt a lot, especially to ensure that potential customers never again had to queue for hours, in vain. It gave us the confidence to mount the national festivals which followed.

However I, like many, mostly remember the fun of being involved. I'm sure that nobody who was there on the Saturday night will forget the whole hall ringing with the song "If you hate Watney's, clap your hands". Real ale was certainly alive and kicking at Covent Garden.

John Bishopp

THE RIGHT TO KNOW

"CHOICE BASED ON accurate information is a prerequisite for the consumer in a democratic society." With these somewhat pompous but nonetheless welcome words, the Rt Hon Roy Hattersley, then Secretary of State for Prices and Consumer Protection, opened the Second Great British Beer Festival at Alexandra Palace in 1978. As the First Great British Beer Festival at the same venue had been opened by Terry Jones of Monty Python and Penrhos Brewery fame, CAMRA had come a long way in twelve months!

In terms of the approximate alcoholic strengths of beers, Mr Hattersley was already slightly behind the times. CAMRA's 1976 *Good Beer Guide* had published the original gravities of no less than 304 real beers. In terms of ingredients, British beer drinkers today would still welcome accurate information upon which to base purchasing decisions. After twenty-one years, CAMRA has still not been successful in securing ingredient disclosure. This remains an important campaigning issue for the 1990s.

The campaign for the declaration of original gravities was one of CAMRA's early technical battles. The Food Standards Committee Report on Food Labelling in 1964 had recommended against any requirement for a declaration of the original gravity of beer. The big brewers were most unlikely to volunteer the information as the trend was for them to reduce the gravities, if not the prices, of the beers which they produced.

In 1971 very few data on the strengths of different beers were available, although average beer consumption in the previous ten years had risen from 193 pints/head/annum to 228 pints/head/annum. Frank Baillie's lovely monograph, *The Beer Drinker's Companion* (David & Charles, 1973), briefly discussed the products of 88 different independent brewers with some fairly simple comments.

The national brewers were listed but few comments were offered on their products! The book contained no details on the gravities or strengths of any of the beers.

CAMRA is frequently credited with specifically campaigning against Watneys. The appellation Grotney certainly stuck. But as Michael Hardman has often said, there *was* no specific decision to campaign against Watneys. Watneys merely made stupid mistakes which CAMRA enjoyed exposing. The Barnsley and Stones marches made early headlines, but the backroom work on the declaration of gravities received less attention.

As with much of CAMRA's best work, official and unofficial activities were pursued simultaneously. In April 1974 the Food Standards Committee was asked by the Ministry of Agriculture Fisheries and Food to advise on "the definition, composition and labelling of beer". CAMRA set up a working party to co-ordinate its submission. Later the Committee told me that CAMRA's submission was more thoroughly researched and more thoroughly referenced than any other, including the one from The Brewers' Society. It is interesting to note that, although the Food Standards Committee invited submissions from any interested party, not one brewer, major or minor, made any representation. Frank Baillie did: Tim Amsden did: three County Councils did: ICI, Colmans Foods and ABM Maltings also did, but not one brewer. Everything was left to the Brewers' Society to make a cosy submission in an attempt to ensure a minimal level of interference.

In February 1975 CAMRA was asked to comment on certain possible proposals and to submit supplementary material. The CAMRA Working Party also gave oral evidence. The Report, published in 1977, essentially vindicated all CAMRA's arguments. Although the details of the recommendations were not all to our liking, the overall tenor of the Report was very favourable.

On the subject of beer strength the Report recommended that beers should be designated to be in one of five gravity bands – up to 1035, 1035 – 1041, 1041 – 1047, 1047 – 1062, 1062 and above. Whilst this was a step in the right direction, 82% of beers at that time fell in to the bottom two bands. The other three were, therefore, rather wasted. In April 1977 we repeated to the Ministry of Agriculture Fisheries and Food our view that original gravity $\pm 1°$ remained the preferred option, but if a banding system were to be introduced, a different structure was more appropriate. Further correspondence continued in the summer of 1977, and another oral submission was made in the autumn of that year. Unfortunately the 1979 General Election came before any detailed legislation could be introduced, but, without doubt, CAMRA had won the technical argument.

Meanwhile Michael Hardman's unofficial activities as CAMRA's Editor of Publications had been even more successful. He had regularly asked brewers to declare the original gravities of their beers and teased those who refused this reasonable request. We had a great stroke of good fortune when an analyst working for a major brewer in London became an active member of the Technical Committee. Part of his job was to measure gravities in his laboratory. So long as we did not inundate him with samples, he could slide in a few each week for CAMRA. In this way we built up a database of original gravities. We always gave breweries the results of our analyses and asked them for comment. The 1976 *Good Beer Guide* published the original gravity of each of the 304 real ales listed in the Brewery Section. Those in bold type were published by the brewers themselves: those in light type were figures from a major brewery analyst! None was ever questioned.

Once again Michael's unconventional journalist's approach had obtained the answers first. The combined acitivities mean that, today, most pump clips and almost all bottled beers do contain a statement of the gravity band. I look forward to the day when a short list of ingredients (malted barley, hops, liquor and yeast, preferably) follows!

Chris Bruton

DRAUGHT BURTON ALE

'Black cats', said the marketing man. 'That's what I want this campaign to be about. Black cats.'

As a PR man of the traditional ilk – ex-local newspaper hack and failed Fleet Street wannabe – I was accustomed to marketing types talking in tongues. But what the hell did 'black cats' have to do with anything? Maybe, I surmised, it's something to do with beer drinkers' socio-economic profiles. Or perhaps a secret new ingredient in what they called 'the marketing mix.'

In fact it was neither of these. What my marketing colleague was trying to convey was the need for subtlety in the launch and promotion of a brand new beer, Ind Coope Draught Burton Ale. At the time – spring, 1976 – there was an advertising campaign running which endeavoured to rekindle the public's demand for Craven 'A' cigarettes, the brand which featured a moggy's head on the packet. The ads featured a slinky feline, the copyline: 'Black cats are coming,' and nary a ciggy to be seen. It was all terribly oblique, and a precursor to posters which feature pieces of torn purple silk and abstract bits of Benson & Hedgery.

What my marketing boss required was a plan to launch Ind Coope Draught Burton Ale in a way which avoided the need for big-budget TV ads and huge hollering hoardings. That would have been too overt, too aggressive. PR, he decided, was the key. Set up a few tastings. Get a few pictures into the paper. And, most of all, re-establish Allied Breweries as a credible supplier of traditional, cask-conditioned ale. Be subtle. Be persuasive.

The implications slowly dawned. I was to be the company's torchbearer, lighting Allied's path back from the dark era of keg beer to the salvation of real, cask ale. I'd been working in the St John Street,' EC1 headquarters of Allied Breweries (subsequently rechristened Allied-Lyons) for a couple of years before Burton Ale was conceived. Most of the beers I'd been promoting are listed in the CAMRA Catalogue of All-Time Villainy. Draught Double Diamond, Long Life ('the beer that's brewed for the can') and Skol lager.

Indeed, I can remember attending the launch of *the Good Beer Guide*, and sitting next to CAMRA founder Michael Hardman. As Roger Protz harangued the assembled guests with a vituperative attack on the Big Six brewers, I told Mike I felt like a whore at a nuns' convention.

But then that's what it was like back in the days when nine out of ten pints were keg, and national brands were king. Whitbread Tankard, Watney's Red, DD: that was what real men drank. Consistency was the creed. If a beer tasted the same in Penzance as it did in Paisley, then the brewer had done his job, and everyone would be happy. Everyone, it seemed, but the increasingly vocal platoons – soon swollen to battalions – of CAMRA members.

Allied did, in fact, endeavour to provide some regional variation in bitter and mild with Tetley's in the north, Ansells in the midlands, and Ind Coope down south. But the fact they were either brewery-conditioned or served under top-pressure meant that CAMRA caned the company and its beers mercilessly. And in the 1970's, if anyone in CAMRA so much as broke wind, it was religiously chronicled by the media, both national and local.

So the introduction by Allied of Draught Burton Ale provided a heaven-sent opportunity to demonstrate that the company really *did* possess brewers who cared, knew what they were doing, and could produce a pint of the real stuff which would have drinkers reaching for the superlatives – and another pint, please.

It thus seemed a sound idea to invite senior CAMRA folk to Burton to see for themselves this new wonderbrew. Like proud fathers, I reasoned, it would be splendid for them to be in at the birth. Which is how, early one summer morning in 1976, twenty of CAMRA's leading figures came to be standing on Platform Four of St Pancras station, thirsts and suspicions equally honed. The former was partly satisfied on board the train to Burton-on-Trent with the service of coffee and tea to accompany the excellent British Rail breakfast (despite Graham Lees' gripes about the absence of kippers on the menu). Not sufficiently, though: by 9.30am another member was observed sneaking a slug of something alcoholic but distinctly UNreal from a chilled can.

There was much merry banter on the journey, rather like a bunch of Leeds United supporters en route to a Cup match with Crewe Alexandra. Whisked by luxury coach from the station to the mighty Burton brewery, the party (which, somewhat riskily, embraced a few journalists including a chap from *The Sunday Times*) was in high spirits, and ready to see what new poison the Demon Brewers of Allied were about to wreak upon an unsuspecting public.

Hugely to my relief, the whole occasion went off without a hitch. The CAMRA crew were impeccably behaved – much, I suspect, to the amazement of our hosts – and the Ind Coope folk talked encouragingly about handpumps and regional tastes. The guests were even button-lipped on the tour round the brewery. It seemed inevitable that someone would crack a jibe about the clinically pristine hangar which housed the coppers. But no one did – those first pints of Draught Burton Ale had clearly induced bonhomie and warm fellow feeling.

Since then, of course, the brew has worked similar magic across the land, and by the end of the 1980s was selling 76,000 barrels from 3,000 outlets, with around 500 licensees qualifying for the Ind Coope Draught Burton Guild of Master Cellarmen. And it must have given those Ind Coope brewers a cosy glow of satisfaction when Burton Ale was named CAMRA's Champion Beer of Britain for 1990/91.

So like all good tales, the story of how Allied got back into big-time brewing of cask ale has a happy ending. Which is more than can be said for the train journey back to London for those pioneering CAMRA folk who first sampled Burton Ale.

One celebrated guest – no names, no pack drill, but he writes for the *Daily Mirror* and likes rugby league almost as much as beer – demanded champagne, and feigned high dudgeon when he didn't get it.

Dammit, I thought. He's been giving us stick for months about selling booze which is fizzy, expensive and snazzily packaged. Hold the Lanson – let him drink Long Life!

Richard Harvey

LICENSING HOURS REFORM

FROM THE OUTSET, CAMRA showed a keen interest in and desire for reform of the archaic UK licensing laws. To the vast majority of the public, these laws were totally outdated and inadequate for the demands of modern society. After all, the First World War had ended over 50 years earlier!

By happy coincidence, CAMRA's formation came about just prior to the publication of two major reports on licensing laws, namely the Erroll Report (on licensing laws in England and Wales) and the Clayson Report (on licensing laws in Scotland). Although not entirely in agreement with all of the recommendations contained in these reports, CAMRA was nonetheless active in its support for implementation of the bulk of the reforms advocated.

CAMRA had already formed a "Licensing Committee" that frequently voiced its support for more flexible licensing hours. It lost no time in following up the Erroll and Clayson Reports with MPs, Home Office Ministers and various Government Departments including the DHSS. Meetings of the Licensing Committee were frequently held to monitor the situation, report on progress, and plan further lobbying. Pre-eminent amongst its members was Andrew Cunningham, whose experience and devotion to the subject kept CAMRA's interests alive, not just in those early years but all the way through the campaign to the late 1980s.

A rather strange "bed-fellow" of CAMRA in those days (but only in respect of licensing reform) was the Brewers' Society. It was the most vociferous body in the licensed trade in favour of licensing reform for very good economic reasons. The tourist industry, too, was in favour of liberalisation, as were a sizeable proportion of MPs. The Erroll and Clayson Reports, however, had their critics, particularly the medical associations, temperance bodies, and, of course, that hardy annual "The Lord's Day Observance Society."

Despite these protestations, the legislative authorities in Westminster seemed to favour implementation of the Clayson Report although it was published a year later than the Erroll Report and after the Erroll Report had been effectively shelved. So, in 1976, the Licensing (Scotland) Act came into force and began the process of liberalising Scottish pub hours. At first, evening opening hours were extended and then, gradually, afternoon hours were extended. Eventually licensing hours went from 11.00am to 11.00pm without the necessity of a break except for Sundays which traditionally in Scotland remained "dry." In October 1977, however, the last resistance collapsed and for the first time Sunday pub-opening was allowed in Scotland. During this period of "Scottish" reform, CAMRA was particularly active in promoting not just flexible hours of licensing but provision of real ale in pubs as well. As a result, a number of real ales and small breweries appeared on the scene.

The decision by the Government to allow reform to apply in Scotland and not in England and Wales was perceived by many to be a "trial" exercise before tackling the politically more problematic exercise south of the border. CAMRA's campaign for equal treatment continued, and might have been achieved in the late 1970s if it had not been for a change in Government. The new Government did not hold "licensing reform" amongst its top priorities, so CAMRA was obliged to renew its campaign.

Around this time a growing number of anti-alcohol lobbies arose, amongst whom Alcohol Concern and Action on Alcohol Abuse were particularly active. To some extent these bodies may have been formed as a result of the publication by the DHSS in 1981 of a discussion document entitled *Drinking Sensibly*, which outlined the increase in alcohol consumption and misuse over the previous 20 years or so and aimed to stimulate public debate on the causes and the remedies of this unwelcome feature. To some extent, the anti-alcohol bodies were "front" organisations for the old temperance lobby, which saw the modern preoccupation with health as its best publicity base.

In the early 1980s CAMRA formed a new Committee entitled "Economics, Industry and Government Committee". This immediately adopted a new and revitalised approach to the "licensing reform" campaign. In particular, more emphasis was placed on Parliamentary lobbying and detailed research. Parliamentary activity was stepped up in liaison with various allies, and as a result there were two attempts, by Private Members' Bills, to amend the existing legislation. These Bills, proposed by Rob Hayward MP and Allan Stewart MP, both failed. But the campaign was gathering momentum. CAMRA Branches lobbied their local MPs and CAMRA-sponsored meetings were, for the first time, arranged in the House of Commons.

By now, facts and figures relating to the Scottish experience were beginning to filter through from a spate of surveys and data on key indicators, such as prosecutions for drunkenness and drink-driving. It appeared that licensing reform in Scotland had had few bad effects, and had actually helped to civilise the country's drinking habits.

CAMRA decided to undertake its own surveys of the "Scottish" experience and of opinion in England and Wales in regard to licensing reform. The results of this research, together with a summary of the background to the licensing laws both at home and abroad and CAMRA's own proposals for licensing reform, were published in a report in 1985 entitled *Licence for Change*. The launch of this document took place in the House of Commons and was instrumental in getting the Government finally to take action on licensing reform. The Report became a reference point for not only MPs and Ministers but also for the licensed trade industry and the media.

In August 1987, Government proposals for reform of the licensing laws were published in England and Wales. Although welcome, these did not go as far as CAMRA had proposed, particularly in relation to Sunday opening hours and display of opening times outside licensed premises. The Bill reached Parliament in November 1987. A number of amendments resulted from the Parliamentary process, most notably a one-hour extension on Sunday lunchtime, a change conceded when, it is said, the noble Lord leading for the Government nodded. The Bill received Royal Assent in June 1988, and came into effect on 1 September 1988. So far, few adverse results have been reported, and it is now possible to view England and Wales as being only marginally less civilised than most of the rest of Europe in terms of licensing hours.

So ended one of CAMRA's major and most successful campaigns. One suspects that with the prospect of legislation to legitimise Sunday shopping CAMRA will be once more in action in attempting to reform the pub opening hours on Sunday, the real day of leisure for most of us.

Jim Scanlon

THE RED PLAGUE

'WHAT'LL YOU HAVE, Mike?' I asked my companion, an Army officer-turned-student, as we entered an unfamiliar pub some twenty-one years ago. 'Oh, I don't know,' he replied, heading for the Gents, 'whatever is their keg'.

Of the millions of words spoken on the subject of beer since then, few have been so tellingly evocative, or have encapsulated quite so neatly the bar culture of those far-off days, the essence of that mass-market way of thinking which so nearly prevailed, so nearly eradicated not only the joys of cask-conditioned beer which once again we take for granted, but perhaps a lot else in life besides.

In 1971 there was not much you could do but grit your teeth and buy whatever was their keg, at least for your undiscriminating friend and in many circumstances for yourself, too. Although tied houses of most brewers had a cask bitter and mild, there was alongside it some kind of 'up to date' dispenser, usually a tin box with a light inside, for the house brand of keg bitter. On the brewer's price list (public bar only) this would come first, in big letters or its own style of type face, and it cost sixpence more and therefore must have been superior.

Go to a free house and these things were all you were offered, especially in the holiday pubs of the West Country where Mike made his seminal utterance. Watneys Red Barrel emerged at the bar by courtesy of a dinky plastic barrel with a bulb inside. Whitbread Tankard (mercifully not encountered by Dr. Spooner) was heralded by a dimpled grey pewter-effect drinking vessel with plastic froth on top, and Courage Tavern ('It's what your right arm's for') by a sedate porcelain-look device suggesting a flattened sherry butt. As year succeeded year these objects became less polite and more lurid, positively shouting for attention. An angular blue letter E bawled out the wares of Messrs. Worthington, followed soon after by a vivid red and orange *DD* which rendered up-to-date the hitherto more restrained Double Diamond, which, as you may remember, 'worked wonders'.

Perhaps the most grotesque of these contraptions was the one for Whitbread Trophy, the pint which apparently thought it was a quart – a translucent sports cup which spilled over with plastic whiteness like an elephant's orgasm.

Thinking back to that dismal era it seems that the offence to the eye caused by these garish counter mountings, by contrast with the enduring elegance of the traditional handpump, was of more concern than the offence to the gullet which the beer itself produced. This is partly true, if only because serious beer drinkers went to great lengths to avoid it, developing a taste for barley wine or gin and tonic as a precaution. The characteristic of the grand old kegs of yesteryear was a bland sameness; they were meant to appeal universally and be the same from Land's End to John O'Groats. They were quite rich, fairly sweet, usually over-carbonated, and profoundly dull, stale-tasting and uninteresting, with after-effects ranging from a faintly bilious feeling to a head-banging hangover. It was glutinous on the cheeks and sticky on the bar top. Whatever people drank keg beer for, it certainly wasn't subtlety – it had an old sock mouthfeel and a raspberry in the finish.

One cannot pretend, though, that they were not bought by anyone. People really did drive out to free houses because they sold Red Barrel or Tartan, and one of the earliest of the species, Flowers Keg, was highly spoken of. Many people were impressed by the argument that it was consistent and dependable, unlike the products of some small brewery they might not have heard of. Much of this can be attributed to the aftermath of the Second World War, when beer strength and quality had of necessity sunk to a low ebb. Bottled beers like Worthington or Double Diamond were promoted, and popular, because the brewery could ensure consistent condition even if pubs at that time could not.

People joked that their local brewery had been taken over by Sarsons; the dodgy local beer could be pepped up with a bottle of reputable light ale and from there it was a short step to 'chilled and filtered' or 'canister' beer as keg was variously termed. Neither should we forget the 1960s obsession with modernity and sweeping away the old, be it steam trains, moral values, or medieval houses. When in 1969 Ind Coope introduced a standard policy of CO_2 gas top pressure on cask beer – a kind of halfway house which they thought would ease the transition from cask to keg – they told an eager public that their beers were 'up to date to meet the modern taste'.

In 1970 Watneys came out of the closet and scrapped Red Barrel and its coy suggestion of the familiar and traditional. The dinky, dated barrel was ditched for a bold, upright red keg on the bar. Watneys Red was born, complete with a corporate lettering style and fatuous posters linking such improbable topers as Chairman Mao and Che Guevara with the Watneys 'Red Revolution.' Two years after the Paris student riots, some marketing man presumed they were 'with-it', 'trendy' or the 'in thing'.

What followed was indeed a revolution, of such spontaneity and vigour that no advertising agency might have envisaged. It was a customer backlash, not just against Watneys, but against keg beers and all that went with them. The new beer was only marginally nastier than the old, but the advertising was blatantly absurd, badly misjudged, mistimed, and ill-conceived. The whole presentation, any idea that this was beer, was an insult to the intelligence. Beer had finally been put on a par with baked beans, petrol and soap powder. No longer was it the favourite tipple in the snug, the living tradition of centuries – it was Brand X, your old powder simply wouldn't do. Mrs. 1970s' husband had gone to the pub. People asked you why drinking Watneys was like making love in a punt (answer on p. 579), and 'keg' became an adjective for anything ersatz or naff.

The branded, mass-market, high-tech product was the fulfilment not just of the marketing men's dreams but also of the accountants'. Heeding John Vaizey's monograph which advocated a streamlined, motorway-orientated, modernised industry, and the 1969 Monopolies Commission report which found against the brewers for not having eliminated sufficient outmoded plant, the brewers had merged rapidly and defensively, fearing outsider takeovers, closing clusters of old breweries and building huge computer-driven process plants in strategic if unromantic spots like Luton and Runcorn. Keg was what they needed, not what you wanted.

The gut reaction of Britain's beer drinkers was that Something Had to Be Done, and CAMRA's foundation in 1971 was arguably brought about by the launch of Red. People speak of 'the campaign against Watneys', unaware that there never really was one. In isolated instances, early members were said to have trooped into some benighted keg palace and asked for 'ten pints of real draught bitter'; after ten pints of Watneys had been poured, they made suitably derogatory comments, gleefully refused to pay, and went out. Such antics were heavily frowned on, but no formal tactics were ever devised to oust keg beer.

In one annual report, the Grand Metropolitan chairman spoke of 'a virulent word-of-mouth campaign' which had dented Watneys' sales. There was no such thing; across Britain, thousands of people agreed that keg was horrid and were relieved to discover that it was all right to say so, while CAMRA always led on the positive side, seeking out and advocating good cask beer. Bits of keg-bashing were inevitable; the first commercial edition of the *Good Beer Guide* exhorted drinkers to avoid Watneys 'like the plague' while Bill Tidy's Kegbuster strip, featuring its improbable flatcap hero, did battle with the Grotney's Hard Men. Only the more paranoid hard men of the industry, like the late, overweight pear millionaire Sir Keith Showering thought there was anything dastardly going on and that Chairman Mao's red revolutionaries were actually under his mash tun.

But the writing was on the wall for keg and top-pressure bitters, and within only five years of our foundation it was clear that market domination would not occur. By 1976 big brewers were reviving handpumps and introducing new cask beers rather than risk continuing public vilification. But the existence of a mass market which could be sold more or less anything by television advertising was proven beyond doubt, and if keg bitter was not the product, something else must be found. Fortunately the Big Six had something up their sleeve. Keg bitter begat draught lager.

Brewers had plugged away at lager for decades without much success (except in Scotland, where pouting pin-ups on the can had played a part) in the belief that one day Britain would be much like the rest of the world. Indeed the creation of United Breweries, forerunner of Bass Charrington, was largely based on the exploitation of new markets for Carling Black Label. Given a few hot summers and holidays on the Costa Brava we might get the habit, and something even weaker, higher priced and utterly modern could be mass-produced and marketed just as keg had been. In went the conical fermenters, on went the telly ads – 'there's a terrific draught in here' – and out went the discredited Reds and DDs, brewers hurriedly admitting that they had never much cared for them. Keg bitter was, as the erstwhile CAMRA chairman and writer Christopher Hutt so memorably put it, a 'busted flush'.

While we rooted for real beer, the Big Six rooted for lager, and the booming beer sales in the late 1970s helped us both; keg bitter went down the pan. It has resumed its rightful place as a convenience beer, a poor man's draught, which satisfies a genuine need for beer by the pint in places too small to stock it by the cask. Drunk by seedy, balding reps approaching retirement, it is sometimes quite palatable on the basis of 'any port in a storm' and even compares favourably with certain lacklustre cask beers if that is not heretical to admit. But the brewers' and the customers' interest has moved on. Foiled in their bid to have us all drink keg, big brewers hope to Fosterise the world. Waking from a nightmare where bitter tasted of carbonated cardboard, customers find real beer is alive and kicking. Even Mike was converted, and probably plumps for 6X.

Tim Amsden

THE PROFESSIONAL TASTE

ON A WINTER'S day of numbing coldness in the late 1970s I stood in the old stone buildings that housed the Penrhos Brewery hard by the Welsh border and drank the finest beer in the world. Jones's First Brew was named after Monty Python star Terry Jones, who had put up most of the cash for the small brewery set in part of a breathtaking half-timbered Elizabethan manor house. The ale that honoured his spirited attempt to start a micro-brewery in such a remote area came fresh from the cask. It was too cold but the aromas and flavours of rich malt and peppery hop bounced through the chill and left memory scars on my tastebuds.

The 1980 edition of the *Good Beer Guide* described Jones's First Brew as 'malty and lightly hopped'. The description was inaccurate and did not begin to pay respect to the beauty of the beer. I can hardly complain, because I was editor of the guide at the time, but democracy decreed that beer descriptions were left to the local CAMRA members.

Now all I have is the memory of that beer, for the brewery soon went out of business, its manager, Martin Griffiths, driven to despair by his inability to find outlets in a region where the 'free trade', even the local police club, was handcuffed through loans to Whitbread.

Describing the myriad tastes of beer was a rudimentary business in the early days of the Campaign. The beer we liked and fought to save was brown in colour and ran the full gamut from 'sweet' to 'hoppy'. If you became too poetic about a pint you were advised by the CAMRA hardmen to 'Get it down yer neck'. Beers in the 1980 GBG were 'pleasant', 'sweet', 'full flavoured' and 'unusual'. As late as 1986, with Neil Hanson in the chair, ales still passed muster with such soubriquets as 'well rounded' and 'beautifully balanced', which conjure up images far removed from beer to my Politically Incorrect mind.

It was not until the 1990 edition, edited by Andrea Gillies, that beers started to get descriptions that went beyond the fleeting and the subjective and paid some respect to the skills of the brewer.

But change had been on the way for some time. Even as I drank at Penhros in those far off days, Michael Jackson was traipsing through Europe and North America and garnering knowledge from brewmasters and connoisseurs. He sent messages back to a largely disbelieving British audience that lager beers had a heritage as proud as ale's and should not be judged by the risible imitations being foisted on the British market.

Lager, ironically, was the catalyst for change in the way in which the CAMRA cognescenti approached and enjoyed beer. As we made our first faltering forays into Germany and Czechoslovakia we found that Jackson was right. Here were beers – and nobody in those countries called them lager – that had aroma, palate and finish redolent of malt and hops instead of the fizzy metal polish we found in the likes of Harp and Skol. In a village high in the Austrian Alps, a tiny brewery produced a Pils that I swear tasted like a colder version of Joseph Holt's legendary Manchester bitter. I immediately abandoned all my conceptions and followed in Jackson's giant footsteps.

Brewers became less reticent when they discovered that CAMRA was not the pestilential nuisance portrayed by the disinformation bureau of the Brewers' Society. The Campaign's writers and technical experts were genuinely keen to know how beer was made. Michael Hardman's lyrical exposition of the brewing process in *Beer Naturally* showed that CAMRA was about more than just sinking eight pints a night in the Frog and Nightgown – though, in order to preserve his reputation, it must be stressed that Hardman managed both writing and consumption with awesome dedication.

Many questions needed to be answered. Why did beers vary so enormously in taste and character? What were the differing but interconnected and overlapping contributions made by malt, hops, yeast and water? What role do "adjuncts" play in brewing? What are the real differences between ale and lager?

The inquisitors were aided enormously by the arrival of Dr Keith Thomas and his Brewers' Laboratory. Brewlab has had a peripatetic existence, based in the City of London Polytechnic, then North London Polytechnic and now Sunderland University, but managing all the while to explain the mysteries of fermentation and faults in finished beer to both brewers and lay drinkers. Thomas is a scientist with a welcome ability to explain the arcane rituals of brewing in simple terms. He is also a brewer of distinction. His Flag Porter is not just based on an 18th century recipe but is fermented with a yeast found in a bottle of porter rescued from a shipwreck; Thomas painstakingly recultured the yeast and let it loose on modern malts.

Knowledge came thick and fast now. The single most important strand came with the understanding that even if two brewers, cheek-by-jowl, use identical varieties of malt, hops and local spring water, their beers will still be sharply different as a result of the yeast strains used. Yeast is more than a fungus that turns a sugary solution into alcohol and carbon dioxide. As it is used, cropped and re-used for years, decades and even centuries it will soak up the characteristics of its brewery, helping to impart distinctive flavours to the beer.

Remove the yeast from that brewery and transfer it elsewhere and it will change the character of the beer in its new home within a brew or two. At the most extreme, an ale yeast set to work in the conical fermenters of Charles Wells' high-tech brew house in Bedford will transform itself into a 'bottom' lager-type strain but will still produce a beer that is definably ale. Yeast strains are carefully logged and stored in a special yeast bank in Norwich. A new brewer keen to replicate, say, the lightly fruity and sulphury ales of Burton-on-Trent could take a bucket round to Marston's, but is more likely to make a trip to Norwich.

The difference between lager and ale is more profound than just the use of top and bottom yeasts. During ale fermentation, which takes place at a warm temperature of 15 to 25 degrees Celsius, the rapid speed of the conversion of sugar to alcohol creates a vast army of fruity esters. Walk into the fermenting room of any ale brewery and your senses will be assaulted by ripe and tempting aromas of apple, orange and blackcurrant. These flavour characteristics will be less dominant in the finished beer and, during the short conditioning period that follows fermentation, the brewer will purge rough esters that he considers undesirable.

But, due to the use of robust pale ale malt, darker and more vigorously kilned crystal malt, and perhaps even a touch of dark chocolate malt, an ale will deliver a fascinating range of aromas and flavours, from the light citric fruitiness of Tetley Bitter, through the orange twang of Adnams, the Cooper's marmalade of Ind Coope Burton Ale, and the bitter coffee of bottled Guinness, to such improbable but clearly present characteristics in high gravity beers as leather and creosote in Courage's Imperial Russian Stout and ripe pineapple in Traquair House Ale.

I have spotted a definite gooseberry note in Belhaven's splendid 80 shilling ale and a hint of banana in Eldridge Pope's Royal Oak. Boddingtons Bitter, despite its modest strength, is an ale of enormous complexity. The head brewer finds brandy notes on the nose while I settle for lemon jelly and spices.

Such flavour characteristics are avoided by the true lager brewer. During the long conditioning (lagering) period – up to three months for Budweiser Budvar – most of the fruity esters will disappear, leaving light but delectable honey and vanilla notes from a malt that is usually much paler than the type used in classic pale ale brewing.

Without hops, beer of any type would be unacceptably malty. For British ale brewing, fertilised hops are used. The classic varieties, Fuggles and Goldings, impart an earthy bitterness and a peppery, herbal aroma. The unfertilised female hops favoured by lager brewers give a more gentle bitterness – though when the units of bitterness rise to forty, as in the Czech Pilsner Urquell, there is no doubting the impact of the climbing weed that shares the same family as both the nettle and cannabis.

The growing awareness of the subtleties and complexities of brewing had an impact within CAMRA and its publications. At first many members shied away from analysis of aroma and taste that seemed redolent of the snobbery and absurd 'absolute mangoes' manifestations of the wine tasters. The expression 'chocolate notes', which stressed the impact of roasted malts in stouts and old ales, caused particular offence to those who felt that such arty-fartiness took beer out of the pub and into the yuppy wine bar.

But the sudden, late 1980s boom in sales of cask beer made such grumbles seem inappropriate. Suddenly even the tabloids were taking beer seriously and it was possible to both wear a metaphorical cloth cap and discuss the 'mouth feel' of your favourite bitter. CAMRA's Technical Committee, set up originally to look at such matters as good cellar practice and dispense methods, took on a more central role. Working closely with Keith Thomas, the committee turned the annual Champion Beer of Britain competition from a haphazard affair into one in which judges were schooled in such matters as head retention, lace work, nose, palate and finish. The committee also organised seminars for *Good Beer Guide* inspectors, whose tongues were 'profiled' by the energetic Dr Thomas. As a result, out went well-rounded and beautifully balanced beers from the guide, to be replaced by descriptions that more accurately unravelled the fusion of malts and hops.

This work will continue and grow more professional: as David Hart, managing director of Hall and Woodhouse, said in 1992, 'CAMRA is no longer just a reactive body but is one based on connoisseurship'.

I suspect that appreciation of the skill of the brewer will ultimately annoy a few of them, though, for a deeper understanding of the art will begin to ask more and more questions about ingredients. Few beers are all-malt. Wheat, maize and different forms of sugar are widely used and are likely to be challenged in the 1990s. CAMRA, from time to time, has toyed with demanding that British ale should be brewed to the same strict purity law as Germany's Reinheitsgebot. It is not achievable and the benefits are doubtful: there is a world of difference between a beer lagered for three months at zero temperature, purging itself of rich fruit notes, and an ale produced rapidly by warm fermentation that is expected cheerfully and proudly to proclaim its fruitiness. That should not mean, however, that British beer drinkers should have to put up with near beers made, in the case of Whitbread's Cheltenham brews, from just seventy-two per cent malt, the rest of the specification comprised of torrefied wheat (popcorn) and sugar.

The respected head brewer of Harvey's of Lewes says the use of cereal adjuncts allows him to 'play tunes' with his beers. They are pleasant liquid melodies but, in the wrong hands, adjuncts can produce silly symphonies. As ingredients listing approaches, consumers will be aware for the first time that beer is not a simple bucolic drink that comes straight from the barley field and hop farm. Faced by the information that many beers are propped up by substantial amounts of sugar and that some erstaz lagers contain as much papain and rice grits as malt, consumers will undoubtedly demand that the brewers clean out their mash tuns and coppers.

CAMRA will play a leading role in such a campaign. I would be happy to see the adoption of a simple demand that cask ales should contain not less than ninety per cent malt: simple but it would cause a deal of consternation in a few board rooms.

The appreciation of beer has come a long way in CAMRA's short life. It may come to be seen, along with the preservation of independent brewers, as its most enduring contribution to Britain's unique style of brewing. But appreciation and knowledge have their limitations. Nothing will ever bring back the taste of Jones's First Brew, a beer that in the finest traditions of Monty Python made you walk in an extremely silly way after a pint or three.

Roger Protz

BATEMAN'S

THIS OCCASION LEADS my mind to wander back to the time of my own 21st birthday. I was then a brewing pupil at Kelsey's of Tunbridge Wells, subsequently Whitbreads, and Green's of Luton, subsequently Flowers then Whitbreads. In addition to ourselves there were still five other breweries in Lincolnshire – Sargents's of Brigg who belonged to Hewitts, Hewitts of Grimsby who eventually became Bass, Soulby Sons & Winch of Alford who joined Mowbrays of Grantham and sold out to Flowers, and Soames of Spalding, who went to Steward & Patteson of Norwich and then to Watney.

Bernard Dixon, my brewing mentor, was at the forefront of amalgamating local breweries into regionals, and offered to me the Managing Directorship of a new Lincolnshire brewery to be built near Grantham, but the prospect did not entice me as it ignored another member of the family and Batemans lived on.

We had some 70 village pubs, and in most places there was also a Soulby and a Soames. Our salvation came in 1957 when we crept in through the back door on a deal between Steward & Patteson and Flowers. The outcome was the sale to us of all the ex-Soames and ex-Soulby village pubs north of Boston, together with a few in Boston as sweeteners, but sufficiently run-down for us to be able to afford. Twenty-nine houses for £50,000 sounds a real snip now, but in 1957 it was absolutely impossible to borrow that sort of money anywhere due to the Government's very strict credit squeeze, which prevented banks and insurance companies from making any loans. I shall always be grateful to an anonymous friend in the Trade who gave us the temporary assistance that was so essential to us.

My father said that the renovation and rationalization of these pubs would keep us occupied for at least eight years, and I promised myself not to purchase a new car until every one had a bathroom – which happened in five.

When I joined Batemans after Army and pupillage my father had only just about completed the backlog of pub repairs due to the Second World War on a scheme of tax allowance known as Deferred Repairs, and very many of our houses were still 6-day beer-only licences. I spent much of my time in Court with maps, petitions and plans getting these up-graded to Beer and Wine and eventually Full Licence. It is interesting to remember that most of our pubs had no counter as "Perpendicular Drinking" was considered one of the deadlier sins before the War. Also, by law, one could not have a full licence without two rooms – presumably the labourer should not be corrupted by seeing his master drinking whisky.

On the brewing side we were until 1953 carrying out all our fermentations in the carriage cask, that is to say in every size from pin to hogshead that was expected to be required in trade. The casks were stacked on pine troughs in such a way that the fermenting beer would flow out of the bunghole and down the belly of the cask, and was topped up by can from the trough every two hours day and night at the peak of the fermentation. The full horror of this will be apparent when I say that this was carried out in ground floor rooms where the heat of fermentation took the temperature up to 80°F in the summer – we did at least whitewash the slate roofs every spring!

We installed a refrigerated air-conditioning plant in 1951 and that, together with the felling of my fruit trees and the lovely old pear tree on the brewery wall as they might have caused wild yeast trouble, saved us in the nick of time.

The cask washing also was somewhat primitive. It depended on rumbling by hand with hot water and chains, beaten flat by the blacksmith, in order to scour the yeast off the cask, which was particularly hard because of the fermentation. My first project was to put in a steam jet to sterilize the casks (insofar as one could with old oak) and then to set about planning the installation of fermenting vessels.

Before doing this I needed to have some reassurance that the character of our beer would not be adversely affected by stainless steel, particularly as there was a strong school of thought that considered the formation of beerstone on copper vessels to be essential to the formation of CO_2 bubbles to assist the yeast in rising. A number of brews in 50 gallon yeast tubs convinced us we were on the right track, and 8 gleaming stainless steel vessels replaced our old carriage cask system in 1953. The attemperators were made of a special steel to withstand the salt of our borehole, which after a few weeks had found a channel straight from the North Sea, but the iron content caused galvanic action so we went on to recirculated refrigerated water for our air-conditioning plant.

The next spectre looming was Watney's Red Barrel and the prospect that all draught beer in the future might be in what is now called brewery-conditioned form. To this end we built ourselves a "Heath Robinson" keg washer and filler and were more successful with our version of a keg beer than was convenient at that time. We were having increasing difficulty in convincing our tenants that draught beer containing yeast was preferable to the filtered version. This was particularly so as sales of draught had dropped to the extent that we were beginning to use ¼-pint Simcup and Dalex Pumps in the place of ½-pint beer engines. I was even proud to have proved that a little Dalex would pull beer from an eight-foot-deep cellar.

This must have been around 1971, and I was very conscious of the fact that we could not fight a rearguard action much longer to hold back the tide of demand from our tenants for our keg beer which would have meant an investment in containers, packaging and dispense equipment far beyond our means. At this critical moment, as the sun might well have been setting on Batemans, yet again there appeared a knight in shining armour in the form of CAMRA.

Quite suddenly and dramatically the old beer engine was an essential piece of equipment in every self-respecting pub and Batemans could hold high the foaming head of Good Honest Ales.

Since those days the association of CAMRA and Batemans has been a very close one – through our battle for Independence and Victory celebrations to brewing CAMRA's special 21st Birthday Ale.

George G. Bateman

Footnote...
In the issue of *The Brewers' Journal* of 20 September 1961, a feature on Bateman's concluded with these prophetic words: "The enthusiasm shown by Mr George Bateman is one guarantee that the brewery at Salem Bridge will go from strength to strength. The quality of the beer you get under the sign of 'Good Honest Ales' is another." *(Editors).*

A SENSE OF PLACE

Twenty years ago keg beer bestrode the market. Brewers saw Double Diamond and Watney's Red as brands with a golden future. Early CAMRA campaigners saw them as weak, bland, poor quality substitutes for the real thing. Within a few years they had passed from the scene, unmourned if not forgotten.

The beer market now stands poised on the brink of another seismic change. After two decades of huge growth, Carlsberg, Heineken and other brands of pouring lager are going into a decline which could match that of their keg predecessors. This scenario, which has already started to happen, is not yet publicly recognised by the national brewers. But recession-hit customers have rumbled the fact that the weak, mediocre branded lagers purveyed so profitably by all the nationals are not worth the 15-20 pence per pint premium they have commanded in pubs.

Contrary to media portrayal, the vast majority of drinkers in the key 18-25 year age group are not oiks and yobs. The lager lout image, which was at its peak in the build-up to the 1990 World Cup, did untold damage to popular national lager brands. These are now shunned by many young drinkers who seek to dissociate themselves from elements which they deplore just as much as older generations do.

Premium draught lagers, stronger and better crafted than pouring brands, are rapidly gaining ground. Designer bottled lagers are surging forward even faster. Within the last two years, Sol has become a 'must stock' item for licensees along with Holsten Diat and Guinness. Stout sales, too, are reviving as Beamish, Murphys and others add variety to the sector.

Real ale is also a beneficiary of lager disillusion. Prospects for growth in sales are better than they have been for a generation. A firm grasp of the changed dynamics in the market place is vital. These changes will bring great gains to some brewers and some brands, but will also lead to the death of others.

Everyone knows that implementation of the M&MC Report was a botched job. Consumers will not, in the long term, benefit either from a wider choice or from lower prices. What has begun to happen, though, is that their local pub is more likely to stock brands they actually want to drink. Allied pubs in the South-east serve Adnams and Greene King rather than the thin gruel of Ind Coope bitter. Greenalls have relented from the uphill task of persuading drinkers to accept their mediocre (Shipstones excepted) brands of bitter and lager, and have stopped brewing altogether.

National brewers will be responsible for many real ales whose sales will surge. In a more competitive free trade, being able to offer an attractive range of real ale is a vital component of the salesman's portfolio. Some of the work the nationals are doing in this field is bogus, some of it deserves vigorous support.

A different critique is needed by real ale drinkers. For many years the important question was 'Who owns the brewery?' This needs replacing by the question 'How and where do they brew the beer?' Integrity of production and source is tomorrow's issue, where yesterday's was ownership of the mash tuns.

Draught Bass has always been a fine real ale, particularly appreciated in the free trade in South Wales and the West Country. For twenty-five years it received no promotional or advertising support. Tenants at one time were actively dissuaded from stocking it. For their recent change of heart, Bass deserve a prodigal son's welcome home. To move production of another unique Burton brand, Worthington White Shield, to Sheffield and then Birmingham is, on the other hand, a more typical example of national brewers' cynicism.

Where any alcoholic drink is made matters a lot. It impacts on palate and flavour in a variety of subtle ways. The producers and merchants and customers of wine and whisky, cognac and champagne recognise this key fact. Why does the British brewing industry seek to ignore it?

Edradour is the smallest distillery in Scotland. It is owned by Pernod/Ricard, the third largest spirits company in the world. The integrity of traditional methods of production and maturation in this small plant is unswervingly supported by the multi-national owner. Compare this approach with that of Scottish and Newcastle, who brew most of their Theakston's production in Newcastle rather than Masham. The discerning consumer of the 1990s will not be taken in for very long by this shabby marketing exercise.

Boddington's Bitter is fine beer, even though it is not the same beer I drank after cricket matches twenty-five years ago. I am amused to see it advertised as 'the Cream of Manchester', pleased that it's available round the corner from where I live in Cambridge, and delighted that production has doubled in the last two years. What really matters is that traditional production standards are maintained and that the brew does not leave its Strangeways home. As long as they treat Boddington's like Pernod/Ricard treat Edradour, Whitbread deserve support not opprobrium.

Many regional brewers are making encouraging progress. Marston's installation of a new set of Burton Unions to handle increased Pedigree production was splendid news. Wolverhampton and Dudley broke new ground with stylish ads for draught mild on regional television. Greene King IPA has become a top selling bitter throughout the south east.

Adnams, Wadworths, Timothy Taylors, are making giant strides in many regions, welcome wherever they go. For other local brewers the right course will be to concentrate on their home territory. These are the people who used to say their beer didn't travel. I suspect the point is more psychological than technical. A pint of Jennings tastes best in a whitewashed hillside Cumbrian pub with panoramic views; Donningtons Bitter is most welcome in a cool Cotswolds taproom with a stone-flagged floor.

The link with place or region is vital to micro-brewers too. It strikes me that some of the most successful are those who have made their beer synonymous with an attractive part of the country, often a tourist district. It's helpful to licensees to be able to offer a unique local pint to visitors keen to experience the spirit of the place. Examples of this approach successfully executed are Exmoor ales in Somerset, Woods of Wistanstow in Shropshire, and Woodforde's whose Wherry Bitter goes down well on the Norfolk Broads.

From Bass to Woodforde's Wherry, all these brewers share a common factor. They are bringing energy and enthusiasm to the production and promotion of real ales which are attractive and enjoyable to free trade customers. Whether the scale is huge and national, or tiny and local, is irrelevant. They deserve support for their enterprise as long as integrity of production and source is maintained.

There is another side to this coin. Many real ales taste insipid, many brewery owners and managers are complacent and lacklustre in their approach to market challenge. It is no part of CAMRA's function to prop up these brands and companies against the force of competition. If some breweries expand in a static market, others will be forced to close.

At some stage, implementation of the M&MC Report will be officially reviewed. The balance of market forces favours huge breweries which achieve economies of scale in production. A healthy market needs new entrants to replace those forced out by competition. To stand a real chance of thriving, the valiant and vital micros need a sliding scale of excise duty below, say, 100,000 barrels a year. Much of the harm that has been done by the botched implementation of the M&MC Report could be corrected by this simple and inexpensive measure.

If that campaigning objective is secured, real ale drinkers can look forward to a golden age where the beer pumps froth and foam with tasty native brews.

Christopher Hutt

THE FULLER VIEW

THE 1960s WERE depressing times for many regional and small brewers. The tidal wave of keg beer, spearheaded by Watney's Red Barrel, was sweeping the country and cask conditioned ale, much of it of dubious quality, was being forced out of the market. Many brewers were spending money they could ill-afford on modernising their plant to cope with the new style of beer, unaware that they were sacrificing their heritage for a trend and were laying themselves open to takeover.

The emergence of CAMRA was the point that started to change the real ale brewers' fortunes. Here was a growing body committed to quality real ales, served through traditional handpumps. The Beer of the Year awards and annual Festival have now grown into a major event and were of enormous benefit to those who participated and won awards. They have helped to make the drinking public aware of the choice that is available throughout the country and at the same time have forced the real ale brewer to look at the quality and consistency of his product.

The public image of CAMRA has also changed. It has now become a more professional organisation which is prepared to comment on any aspect of the brewing industry. In some areas it has been controversial.

In 1989 the Monopolies and Mergers Commission produced the long awaited report on The Supply of Beer. Both the large brewers and the regionals spoke with one voice as they could see that although the aims may have been understandable the recommendations that were put forward would not work. CAMRA disagreed with this viewpoint. Despite talks with regionals they did not appear to appreciate the likely outcome if the recommendations were introduced. Three years later everyone can look back and see how flawed the report was. The market share of the big brewers has increased rather than decreased as they have tied up distribution deals with the new large retailing groups. Those regionals without strong brands are struggling and some may be forced to stop brewing and become retailers with the consequent loss of many traditional brews – not something that CAMRA would like to see at all.

However, for those with strong brands there have been opportunities. The swing back to real ales has once again saved many companies from extinction. Now that quality problems have been addressed, the customer knows that today's cask conditioned beers are consistently better than in the past. Distribution deals have been set up and what were once regional or local ales can now be drunk all over the country.

The fight for market share has, however, become much more competitive and CAMRA should always bear in mind the increasing commercial pressure on breweries both large and small. If companies are to survive they do need to rationalise and in certain instances this has led to closures. Unfortunate though it may be, keeping an unprofitable plant open can make breweries much more vulnerable to takeover.

As well as their tremendous success with real ales, CAMRA have also played an important role in the development of pubs themselves. The annual awards for pub design, which have never received the coverage they deserve, provide an incentive to small brewers to refurbish sympathetically. Pubs should complement the ales which are served in them and fit in with the area. Quality is the keyword and CAMRA should be complimented on their efforts. The days of the same interior design scheme springing up around the country are numbered and as a result of pressure from customers, designers are now given more of a free hand.

Once the pub is right and the beer is right, people need to be told and this is where the *Good Beer Guide* has excelled. It has become the bible for beer lovers. Not only does it give detailed information on all the brewers but more importantly on their best pubs, mixing frankness and good humour ("nice pub, shame about the landlord" was noticed in one year's edition – the landlord is no longer there!). One important result of having not only a national guide, but also its local offsprings, is that the little unspoilt country pubs have been put on the map (and probably in some cases saved from closure) by travelling beer-lovers looking for their own perfect pub.

In short, CAMRA over the years has done a tremendous amount for the regional brewers both directly by supporting their beers and indirectly by promoting the best pubs. It has sometimes been criticised for straying away from its original aims and on occasion rightly so. But any national consumer organisation needs to have discussions and debates on the way forward. At all levels members have worked tirelessly to promote their ideals and as such it has become a club as well as a pressure group. Iain Dobson's MBE in the recent honours list reflects just how far the organisation has come since its early days when it was just a small voice fighting in a corner to keep traditional beers alive. The regional brewers have a lot to thank CAMRA for over the years, as without them some of us would just be names in the brewing history books.

Anthony Fuller CBE

STARTING FROM SCRATCH:
THE NETHERGATE STORY

I COMMENCE this monumentous *(sic)* piece of literature in the wake of the celebration of six years of existence of our Brewery. It was in August 1985 that I forsook academic life in Cambridge in order to set up what for a fair percentage of the male population of this country can only be a dream, namely, a brewery. It took a good seven months to actually gather the plant together and plan things properly, and from March 1986 onwards time seems to have flown by.

My love affair with beer commenced at an age which the judicial system in this country forbids me to divulge. It was in Exeter that I was introduced to our wonderful fermented product; Heavitree Ales, I seem to recall, started the romance. My early years as a football fanatic meant that there was much travelling throughout Great Britain and it was remarkable that we used to know where we were by the local brews advertised in the football grounds and in the match programmes. If it was Hewitt's you were in Grimsby; if it was Massey's you were in Bolton, and so on. Each opposing team could be associated with a characteristic brew. Then disaster! Everyone knows the story of the mass takeovers in the brewing industry. The miserable products emanating from the increasingly expanding mega-breweries horrified enough of us in the early seventies to provide the stimulus for CAMRA. Some were far-sighted enough to actually found the Campaign. Some, who had just started new appointments, had the ideal firmly implanted, but insufficient time to participate actively. I count myself as being in the latter category.

The early Cambridge Beer Festivals were a tremendous stimulus, however. Highly innovative with some wonderful characters involved. It was during those early CAMRA years that I resolved to become actively involved in the brewing industry. Being part of an influential consumer group is one thing; altering things from the 'inside' is another. I have always enjoyed a challenge and favoured the latter route. Little did I realise the extent of the 'challenge.'

My academic duties evolved such that I was responsible for all Industrial Microbiology taught in the syllabi. With a trend towards the new scientific disciplines such as biotechnology, why not concentrate on the oldest form of science, such as food and beverage fermentations? It all seemed so obvious and in total accord with my ultimate aim. After discussing cheese-making, bread-making and other non-alcoholic topics, we soon became ensconced in brewing in all its forms. Courses were liberally served by industrial visits, which are an essential part of any Industrial Microbiology course! We became familiar visitors to Paine's of St Neots and Everard's of Burton-on-Trent. The many happy hours spent at these establishments helped to concentrate my mind, if "concentrate" be the correct word!! I cannot possibly over-estimate the help and encouragement given to me by Wally Pateman of Paine's and by Geoff Calderbank of Everard's. Both were eager to impart any relevant information and both were over-generous with their time and hospitality.

Sadly, Wally passed away in December 1991 and in some ways I would like to think that the Nethergate Brewery is a lasting tribute to him and his ideals. One that Wally impressed upon me is that being a brewer would mean that the job demanded twenty-four hours per day, seven days per week attention. Saccharomyces cerevisiæ has no respect for weekends or Bank Holidays! How right Wally was.

The brave pathfinders of the micro-brewery revolution such as Selby Brewery Co and Litchborough Brewery had the best wishes of us all to help them on their way, but as we all know, sentiments help little in such a cut-throat environment. Some of the early 'micros' have survived, some have perished. It was obvious that not only did one have to brew a good, acceptable, product, but one had to be able to run a business as well. Many of the early new-wave breweries could not make a happy marriage between the two essentials – with the concomitant results. Fortunately a good number are still with us; and doing very well, at that.

My ideas on brewing beer have always been highly traditional and somewhat conservative. I believe that beers should be brewed rather than blended or concocted. Individual recipes should be used and they should consist of malted grains, hops, yeast and water. Colourings, sugars and syrups should be avoided at all costs. It was with these ideals in mind that our Brewery in Clare was conceived and constructed, all equipment for the 10 barrel brew-length plant being supplied by the doyen of the small-brewery revolution, Peter Austin (then at Ringwood). My partner, Dick Burge, is a successful businessman and between us we felt that we had the correct chemistry to succeed.

As with all new companies, it has taken time and great effort to make any impact on the market, but after six years I feel that we are now established and actually getting somewhere. I think that we have now become 'accepted' by the establishment; certainly my participation on the Brewers' Guild training courses would seem to indicate that. Needless to say, our products have been generally enthusiastically received by CAMRA, and we are grateful for that.

We now brew three different beers and for the foreseeable future they will constitute our portfolio. I would love to brew a proper mild ale, but space precludes this at the moment. We could, of course, concoct a mild, but this is not our way of doing things. In fact, I have little time for small breweries that have endless beers on their lists. The discerning customer will know that they cannot all be bona fide brews. Trying to be "all things to all men" is, in my opinion, not the way forward for us 'micros.' I have much admiration for companies such as Butcombe Brewery who have managed to be highly successful with one high class product.

As is the case with the Campaign, we have won some battles, but there are still plenty to be fought. One thing we must not be is complacent. The next year or two will see tremendous changes in the brewing industry. Small breweries, like CAMRA, must be able to adapt. It will be an exciting time and we look forward with confidence. I see the Campaign for Authentic Lager, in some ways an offshoot of CAMRA, as having an important part to play in educating the British public – as CAMRA did in its formative years. With this in mind, we have added a pure German lager (Eichbaum) to our portfolio in the last year and there are encouraging signs that people are beginning to appreciate imported, properly-lagered beer.

The last six years have certainly been hectic and Cambridge now seems light-years away. I still visit there regularly, of course, for we have a number of good outlets in the City – including our first venture into the tied estate business – the Cambridge Blue.

We have encouraged visiting parties to the Brewery, especially CAMRA parties, for we regard such events as being an ideal forum for expounding our ideals. One of the most frequent questions that I get asked is "Why did you leave Cambridge?" Very occasionally I do wonder. Those of you who know me, however, will know the reason! Not all artists are based at Burlington House.

Ian Hornsey

TRUE TO THE YOUNG TRADITION

Youngs OF WANDSWORTH have long shared the values of CAMRA. We were fighting for cask beer a decade before CAMRA was started, and our pubs were already renowned as oases for drinkers of cask beer when the four founders held their first meeting. It is not just values that we share. The term "real" to describe cask-conditioned beer was originally thought up by me to make clear that Young's beer was not keg.

When I began calling our beer "real" there was considerable opposition from the Brewers' Society but I felt strongly that keg beer was so uninteresting that our own cask beer had to be distinguished from it. Keg beer lacks the great charm of real draught beer, which has slight differences from week to week and according to which pub you go to. Real draught beer should always be good, but the slight differences stimulate your tastebuds and your interest.

Keg beers and lagers are hygienically consistent but to my mind they are both boring and dull. I am sure that the reason for the revival in real draught beer today is that people are seeking the exciting difference in taste. The revival is quite incredible. I read economics at Cambridge, and I can recall few examples in economic history where the clock has been put back as it has today. The preservation of what is an important part of the history of this country has much to do with CAMRA and Youngs mutual support in ensuring that cask beer had a future.

We would have found it difficult to survive without the enormous influence CAMRA had and still has. I believe that CAMRA's success stems particularly from the enterprising and influential journalists who managed to have the ear of Fleet Street. The steady flow of attacks against keg beer in their reports succeeded in convincing enough drinkers to seek out real beer.

But they needed breweries to keep producing real beer and to do that companies like mine had to avoid being taken over by the giant brewers. We have a flock of geese at the brewery. I always tell people that we keep them to preserve our independence in the same way they kept predators at bay in Rome in 400 BC. If we had not been independent we would not have been able to stand up against the keg beer trend. Even as an independent brewery it was difficult to make a stand.

One powerful reason why I refused to allow keg beer is that when I first started at the brewery I knew a lot about drinking beer but little about the brewing industry. My father had refused to let any of his children into the business. I went into the shipping business at Newcastle while my other brothers went into such things as banking or the navy. When eventually I started at the brewery in 1954 I was pretty green but this meant that I assessed the situation in the industry with a fresh pair of eyes. What I saw astonished me.

Head brewers took immense time and trouble with their beer at the brewery, ensuring that it left the premises in perfect condition. When it reached the pubs, however, nobody appeared to look after it. The standard of draught beer throughout the country left a lot to be desired. Pubs were often serving beer that was sour or cloudy. Practically all pubs in those days were tenanted (which is a good thing – I am not criticising that) and were therefore individual businesses. There was considerable feeling that the tied trade manager could not interfere too much as long as tenants paid their rent and took the tied beer.

The cellar inspectors did little, even though the beer in the cellars was not up to scratch. They were usually retired draymen and did not have the authority to give stick to tenants who were not cleaning their pipes. The result of the poor quality of draught beer meant that bottled beer became increasingly popular. Eventually the head brewer at Flowers had the idea of putting bottled beer into kegs.

This filtered and pasteurised beer was much easier to keep than normal draught beer and was also less gassy than bottled beer. It was thought to be the solution to all the brewers' problems. At about the same time that keg beer began appearing, the smaller family-owned breweries were disappearing. They were being gobbled up by the big breweries because of death duties and the difficulties in finding suitable heirs. The disappearance of small breweries is similar to the disappearance of family-owned bakeries. The plastic wrapped and plastic tasting bread produced by the big bakeries was swamping the market just as tasteless keg bitter was swamping the pub trade. As the number of breweries dwindled, real beer became harder and harder to find. The breweries that remained followed the keg fashion like sheep.

Since I was new to brewing I was more able to stand against this trend. I opposed keg out of sheer cussedness as opposed to business acumen, with the knowledge that we could either sink or swim by following such a risky strategy. Youngs adopted the attitude that when our beer reached our pubs it should become the pride of the licensee to serve draught beer in tip-top condition. The first step I took was to make the most important people on the staff the cellar inspectors. It was a shock to many when I announced that the cellar inspector should have a company car because in those days the only person who had a company car was the rent collector. Not even the directors had them.

The next sensation came when I gave notice to the tenant of the Horse and Groom in Hampstead because of the standard of the beer being served. The Licensed Victuallers Association was outraged but I was adamant that the tenant's failure to clean his pipes properly was sufficient reason to ask him to leave.

My philosophy concerning keg was most fully laid out in my chairman's statement in our annual report of 1964. It is worth recalling in full:

'We have deliberately abstained from supplying keg beer to our tied houses. Although we admit that there is some custom for keg we have not experienced a demand for it in our houses; on the contrary we have found that we have benefited from concentrating on the perfection of our draught beers, and in particular our Special, aided by the support we have received from our tenants in serving these beers in perfect condition.

'Keg is not draught beer but in most respects a bottled beer in a large *container. It is filtered and by necessity is more gassy than draught beer though less than bottled beer. We do not dispute that it may be more convenient, and unfortunately these days quality is often sacrificed for convenience, but it is also much more expensive. We do not intend to make keg beer available in our tied houses.'*

Only a few years after this statement we were the only brewery in London that still had handpumps in all our pubs and no keg bitter. All my friends at the Brewers' Society thought I had gone mad and they predicted that it would be the end of Youngs. On one much quoted occasion a funeral procession went past the brewery and one wag from another company remarked that I had lost another of my customers. It was a fairly short time, however, before my cussedness paid off.

People began to seek out our pubs because we had a growing reputation for good beer. At one stage we were so overwhelmed by the demand that we had to ration supplies both to our pubs and to people knocking on the door of the brewery. Unfortunately this led to much of our equipment wearing out, particularly our coppers, which had been brewing for over 100 years. The rivets in the vessels were beginning to pop out and there was a danger that the bottom might fall out, too. Experts told us that we had no choice but to rebuild the brewery and recommended that the building took place on a free part of the site so that production could be easily continued during the building work. They also recommended that the equipment should be updated with modern kit such as whirlpools or lauter tuns. Once again, however, I stuck my neck out and made myself unpopular with our brewers by insisting that we should rebuild the brewery with the original, traditional vessels.

If we had abandoned what I call the traditional cooking methods I feared we would go the way of several other breweries and change the taste of the beer. The brewery was rebuilt with each new vessel installed in the place of the old. It was an amazing feat by the architects and the builders. Although we have kept pace with some modern technologies by installing computer operation, we were careful not to replace things unnecessarily. We have a steam-powered beam engine, for example, which dates back to 1835 and is said to be the oldest working one of its type in Europe. It is no longer in regular use but is still capable of driving the mill and the mash tuns. We saw little point in just ripping it out and replacing it with electric motors that would wear out in five years.

There are always people who want to experiment, but it has to be done with caution. When new varieties of hops were introduced to overcome the wilt which had been destroying the hop gardens, brewers rushed to try them out. The new varieties were cheaper and they had a high alpha or bitterness content. The worst of them, however, imparted a flavour and smell to beer which suggested a tomcat had lifted its tail up into your glass.

During a routine inspection of our brewing book one day I discovered to my horror that we had conducted some experiments with these hops. Although it is wrong for a chairman to overide his technical staff I immediately instructed the head brewer to stop experimenting and stick with our traditional Fuggles and Goldings.

Science has much to offer but tradition and expertise also have valuable contributions to make. The family nature of the business at Youngs means that we have much expertise to call on. It certainly means more than the ownership resting with a single family. Amongst our workers we have many families with associations with our firm that go back generations. One family, the Thorns, had been in continuous employment since 1846. Their great-great grandfather worked with my great-great grandfather.

All of these people bring years of experience and expertise in the brewing and keeping of beer. Although we now have laboratories and chemists, there is a great deal to be learned from past traditions and this is one of our key strengths.

It is people and not beer that is our greatest asset. It is the licensee and his staff that make a pub. At one time it might have been true that people went to our pubs because of the beers, but I believe that even in those days the success of a pub depended on the people running it. It is even more the case today.

Respect for people and traditions must also extend to the community in which the brewery is based. Youngs have always placed great importance on our roots in Wandsworth. Our brewery is located on several acres of valuable freehold land. The accountants tell us that it would make financial sense to buy a greenfield site and build a new brewery there. The problem accountants have though is that they find it difficult to measure the value of roots in accountancy terms. I do not believe that we would be able to preserve our traditions or even produce the same sort of beer if we were to move to a new site.

We are part of Wandsworth and belong here. Many of the people that work at Youngs have lived in the borough for years and they all contribute invaluable expertise. Our company has existed since 1831, with brewing on the site taking place since 1675. I hope that the expertise accumulated over that time will not be allowed to die. The future is never certain but the refusal to compromise on our traditions and the considerable support from CAMRA have helped ensure that Youngs will continue well into the next century.

John Young

BAYING AT THE FULL MOON

O N TUESDAY January 8, Wally and Pat Pope closed the door of the Full Moon and set off to start retirement in Bournemouth after 20 years behind the bar.

Not perhaps an especially noteworthy event for any but the regulars of the Buckinghamshire pub, which sports a certificate for 10 years in the *Good Beer Guide*.

But when Wally decided to retire, the brewery, Whitbread, put the 300 year-old local up for sale at a knock-down price of £395,000. The market being as it is, this was promptly slashed to a bargain-basement £330,000.

The brewery maintains that it will do better as a free house, that its sale is part of its normal policy of disposals, and that it is not viable for their purposes. That it is still open under temporary management gives grounds for optimism.

I had better come clean on this story, because I have been in love with this pub from my earliest drinking days and was able to live across the road from it for seven happy years.

I take any threat to it as a deeply personal insult. If they close it down, it will feel as if some giant machine had rolled up this stretch of countryside like a redundant piece of carpet and dumped it, out of sight and out of mind.

"When you have lost your Inns," thundered Hilaire Belloc, "drown your empty selves, for you will have lost the last of England."

Hawridge Common is one of four tiny villages strung out along a narrow lane high in the Chilterns. In medieval times these were densely wooded hills, unpopulated save for bandits.

Over the centuries, clearances were made to allow summer grazing for villages in the vale below, and later came the beech plantations on which the timber and furniture trades of the local towns were based.

Brickmakers, smallholders and the "bodgers" who turned chair legs on pole lathes in the beechwoods made up the sparse population, and only with the advent of the car, and a handful of artistic and literary types who took weekend cottages, did any visitors come here.

Modern services came late to these parts, and main drainage and gas still haven't. The Full Moon is fitted with a bizarre early warning device which emits a continuous bleep – unless it becomes agitated, in which case Wally was supposed to set up a hand-cranked siren in the car park, summoning the villagers to spend their last four minutes in the pub cellar and render themselves oblivious with Winter Royal.

For this was a Wethered's pub, and therein lay a good deal of its attraction for me. The handpumps were never removed, as they had been in most Benskin's pubs, and the crisp and hoppy Marlow beers were sold here continuously from the 1820s when they bought the pub, until 1988, when Whitbread shut the brewery.

The "ordinary" bitter was widely available, partly because CAMRA campaigned for it when Whitbread shut the Chiswell Street brewery in

London, but the SPA or "special" was a rarity, and what a magnificent beer it was!

We lost the mild, but gained the splendid Winter Royal. CAMRA persuaded them to scrap the "Trophy" badge and to be proud of the Wethered's name which had stood the brewery in good stead for more than 200 years.

You could spot a Wethered's pub by certain characteristic alterations, made at the whim of some old-time brewery surveyor who had a thing about metal window frames and extractor fans. If a pub had a big old fireplace he would knock out one side of it, leaving the chimney (and, in this case, half the building) propped up on a metal pole like an overweight Long John Silver.

The Full Moon is further distinguished by low beamed ceilings and a worn stone-flagged floor across which the casks must be trundled to the cellar door. You have to go outside for the lavatories, a practice deemed positively Third World by modern youth.

At the front is is a large old apple tree, a flint wall which soaks up the sun to release it into your luxuriating back of a summer evening, and a view across miles of commons, woods and fields.

In the tidy garden I once supped the length of a morning session with Frank Baillie, author of the *Beer Drinkers' Companion*, who turned up unannounced with an aspiring author named Michael Jackson. The place has refreshed many a CAMRA worthy from John Green to Iain Dobson. Ageing Hampshire hippy Pat O'Neill once dubbed it "the woorrst pub in the woorrld" when he didn't get served at closing time.

The idyll seems to be over. The brewery has gone and "Wethereds" comes from Cheltenham, a cruel parody of a beer, all gushy and flabby. The pub is a lot quieter, thanks in part to the efforts of the local constabulary to persuade people not to drive there from the nearby towns.

The *Daily Telegraph* and Thames TV have both called and written the epitaph, not just of the Full Moon but of the country pub in general.

If it is to survive, it must change, and that which was good enough for 300 years is suddenly no longer good enough. Here is the dilemma for pub lovers, the conflict between sentiment, sentimentality or perhaps selfishness on the one hand, the desire to keep enjoying that enduring, rich contentment that oozes from the fabric of an old and well-loved local, and on the other hand the practicality of running a business in adverse conditions.

The brewery not unnaturally wants to fetch the highest price they can for the property, but they have done the place no favours over the years. Wally Pope was angered by their refusal to consider any worthwhile length of tenancy, under which he might have felt confident to invest his own money.

When he did offer to pay for bringing the lavatories inside, they refused, and when he enquired about buying the freehold, they would not even consider it.

You *could* change the Full Moon without destroying it. It could be extended unobtrusively, to create indoor lavatories, a bigger bar servery and more drinking space.

The food side of it could be greatly expanded and a robust and dynamic licensee could run a highly successful operation. Although we call such places "unspoilt" I doubt if the very first landlord would recognise the interior.

Wally Pope made several discreet changes in the past 20 years which I have to think hard to recall precisely. But while change may be acceptable, it isn't cheap after that hefty purchase price and a lot of beer will need to cross the bar.

Then again, you *could* wreck the place by knocking it through and smearing the walls in wedding-cake plaster, flock wallpaper and adzed beams at demented angles, selling microwaved Golden Duckettes and Webster's Yorkshire Bitter.

The garden could sprout a huge fibreglass teapot, and one might be exhorted to "park prettily" outside "Moonies" wine bar or the "One Small Step" Brasserie.

Failing that you might return in two years' time to find "Full Moon Cottage" prettified with carriage lamps and Austrian blinds and a Colt Shogun in the crisply gravelled drive.

As a mere customer you can but wring your hands and wait while uncontrollable economic and social forces decide its fate.

I used to think Belloc was melodramatic and probably in his cups when he wrote those lines, and drowning never appealed to me much.

Those four final apocalyptic minutes in the cellar with 36 gallons of Winter Royal have acquired a certain period charm.

Tim Amsden

This article first appeared in What's Brewing, February 1991.

SCOTLAND REVIVED

IT WAS ONCE possible to drink a pint in every pub serving real ale in Glasgow and remain stone-cold sober. That's because Glasgow had no real ale pubs at all. Even in the ale-brewing capital of Scotland it was hard to find the kind of beer that made Edinburgh world-famous, because by the early 1970s when the great city of Glasgow was one vast ale desert, almost all Edinburgh pubs had also turfed out decent beer, opting for the cold blast of fizzy keg instead.

That the few pubs in Scotland which remained loyal to real ale were still doing so before CAMRA came on the scene was down to a few stalwarts in the licensed trade, traditionalists who knew how to serve a good pint and whose customers had never forgotten how to drink it. That these people in the beer business were encouraged to carry on and were joined by many others in Scotland is thanks to the efforts of sterling campaigners whose early work to establish CAMRA north of the border laid foundations which are still being built on a couple of decades later.

The handful of ale fans who formed the first tranche of CAMRA membership in Scotland did not dream at the time of what might lie ahead. That after many frustrating years when most of their fellow Scots would continue to sup keg – because there was no alternative in most pubs – it would become difficult to find keg-only boozers in some parts of their country was the aim. The remarkable thing is that it has become a reality. Not only is it hard to discover a keg-only establishment in significant parts of Edinburgh, but a growing number of pubs, notably in Edinburgh but also elsewhere in Scotland, chose to get rid of keg ale altogether during the early 1990s.

Indeed one big brewing business, the Alloa Brewery Company, has atoned for its previous existence majoring on lager, when it brewed no cask-conditioned ale at all, by starting up a chain of non-keg ale pubs called Bert's Bars, where the accent is on real ale, to the approbation of a growing number of thirsty customers (although when Alloa came to open a Bert's in Glasgow they compromised by having a couple of keg taps alongside the banks of hand pumps, just in case Glasgow had not quite forgotten its cask-less past).

Soaring popularity for real ale in Scotland means that it is now available in more pubs than at any time since the 1960s. This is all the more remarkable when it is realised that the keg revolution which is now in retreat began in earnest as long ago as 1962 when Scottish & Newcastle introduced Younger's Tartan Special (a keg ale still widely popular although its sales peaked in 1974). This means that only drinkers aged at least forty-eight can remember a time when all Scottish pubs sold cask.

As well as giving Scotland keg beer, the Sixties provided the country's drinkers with a significantly reduced choice of beers because of a spate of brewery closures and takeovers which raged from 1960 onwards in what was to become known as the locust years, and naff pubs in which to drink what was left because of a craze for trendy alterations which destroyed the character of many traditional bars.

CAMRA's arrival in the 1970s encouraged a revival of consumer choice and retention of those pubs which had survived the mad destroyers of the decade that also gave Scotland's railways the Beeching Axe. The 1970s witnessed improvements, with a better appreciation of good beer and a growth in the number of its outlets, but it was the 1980s before things really got moving with the opening of new Scottish breweries producing cask beer, increased interest in cask by remaining older-established breweries, and pub refurbishments which at least recognised the value of what had gone before. The 1990s have all the hallmarks of being Scotland's decade of real ale and real pubs with proper beer at last available widely from the Borders to the Highlands, in all the cities and in most towns of any size. Not that victory for CAMRA is complete. The position in Glasgow may be so much better, to the extent that it has at last proved possible to publish a guide to real ale pubs concentrating only on that city, but there are still parts of Scotland, including chunks of Glasgow, where cask remains hard to find.

Nevertheless, a great many people have a lot to thank the CAMRA pioneers for. Among those pioneers was Dan Kane, a wonderfully popular figure whose death early in 1992 at the age of forty-five, after months of treatment for leukæmia, was widely mourned. His name lives on thanks to one of the few Scottish independent breweries to survive the locust years, Maclays of Alloa (established in 1830 and whose current brewery dates from 1871). A new, delicious, golden beer bears the proud name Maclay & Co Kane's Amber Ale. How appropriate that Dan's name is on the lips of Scotland's ale-lovers when they order and then savour an ale from a brewery whose survival as a producer of real ale has been helped by the campaigning work he and others in CAMRA in Scotland carried out from the 1970s onwards.

There have been setbacks in Scotland, however. Some of the new breweries did not survive, including the Leith Brewery which was co-founded by Dan's close friend and Scottish CAMRA pioneer, Tony Dean. Leith Heavy is still sorely missed, and is recalled in a surviving advertisement in one of the few Edinburgh pubs which always sold cask beer, even in the evil years of keg domination. This is the magnificently quaint Oxford Bar in Edinburgh's Young Street, which Tony still describes as his local even though he now lives in Belfast. Another of those involved in the Leith Brewery, Ken Garden, has had the recent pleasure of making signs for Edinburgh pubs which are among the growing number returning to traditional decor and traditional ale. If all these outlets had been available at the time, the Leith Brewery would surely have survived.

Other losses have included much older breweries. Just at the time CAMRA was getting started in England, Whitbread dealt Scotland's ale lovers one of the most savage blows ever by closing a brewery they had taken over. This was the Argyle Brewery of Campbell, Hope & King, whose beers were so good they had long held the Royal Warrant. Archibald Campbell had started the brewery in the Cowgate as long ago as 1710 but that did not stop Whitbread – a company which began thirty-two years later than Campbell's – from closing the Edinburgh brewery down. The dons of Edinburgh

University, an organisation which was then just fresh from demolishing some beautiful architecture on the south side of Edinburgh to make way for abominable buildings, were blamed by Whitbread for opposing an expansion plan at the Argyle Brewery, but it is the English company which gained the blame among Scottish beer drinkers. Eventually, in 1992, Whitbread decided to pull out of Scotland after presumably struggling to continue distributing English products at a time when other English brewers – favoured by honest drinkers – have found it worthwhile to benefit from the real ale boom by sending their products north to help quench the thirsts of Scots who twenty years earlier would have dismissed English beer without even trying it.

The historic Argyle Brewery, which incorporates much pre-Campbell's architecture, survives because in twenty-one years no other use has been found for the empty premises. A decade after Campbell's closed, another historic Edinburgh brewing plant closed down, Drybrough's. It went when Grand Met sold its pubs to Allied's Scottish arm, the Alloa Brewery Company, who had earlier taken over many Scottish pubs from Vaux in a deal involving the closure of the Park Brewery of Thomas Usher, a Vaux subsidiary which traded latterly under the name of Lorimer's, a title which strictly belonged to another Edinburgh brewery owned by Vaux – Lorimer & Clark. The one-time Usher's was well into a major modernisation project when the plug was pulled. Had that modernisation been completed, production of Lorimer's Best Scotch, the principal product of Lorimer & Clark, would have been switched to the Park Brewery and the L&C premises would have closed instead.

L&C functioned from the Caledonian Brewery, which had remained virtually unchanged since its opening in 1869 because modernisation never happened due to a belief that the brewery would be shut down. Paradoxically, the decision not to invest in it led to its survival, because by the mid-1980s it had become recognised as a vital part of Scotland's industrial and architectural heritage while in earlier years other breweries had closed in spite of substantial investment.

A near-fatal blow to the Caley (as it is known to its fans, as was the pre-1923 Caledonian Railway which runs alongside) came when Vaux decided that Lorimer's Best Scotch could be recreated in Sunderland. It had been produced entirely for the English market, although some had become available latterly in Scotland as 70 Shilling Ale. Dan Kane, who had been appointed by Vaux to manage the brewery when it added 80 Shilling Ale to its range to help revive a previously-abandoned Scottish market, was among those instrumental in saving the Caledonian through a local management buy-out.

After appearing to struggle for a while the Caley, in spite of owning no pubs of its own, has begun to prosper. Its remarkable range of eight cask-conditioned beers, some of which are also sold in bottled form, has helped make the Scottish beer drinking scene so much better than it has been for many years. The excellent variety of ales from Caley goes a long way to making up for some of Edinburgh's lost beers.

It is no longer possible to savour Aitchison's, Bernard's, Campbell's,

Jeffrey's, Morison's, Murray's, Steel Coulson's, or Robert Younger's ales among others but at least Caley can offer a range of flavours among its all-malt brews, which are made with whole hop flowers instead of the pelletised form of hops now favoured by many breweries. Caley has even cheekily revived a lost brewing name with one of its ales – which was hailed as Beer of the Year by Glasgow and West of Scotland CAMRA branch members. This is R&D Deuchars' IPA, a crystal-clear golden beer with a lovely tang to its "more please" flavour. It's cheeky because there used to be two Deuchars companies, both of which came eventually under Scottish & Newcastle, who neglected to protect the rights to the title. Both original Deuchars companies were based on Tyneside, but one also had an Edinburgh brewery and the other owned a brewery further north, at Montrose.

Belhaven is another independent brewery to survive. It has added a new real ale to its range, St Andrews. This is similar to, but stronger than, their best-selling 80 Shilling. Belhaven also does a cask-conditioned 70 Shilling Ale, based originally on a recipe brewed by Campbell's until 1971. It had come previously from Bernard's, who closed in 1960, but the taste now seems more in keeping with the rest of the Belhaven family than it used to do. Belhaven also does a magnificently malty 60 Shilling, but it is hard to find and most is bottled as "pale ale" (an odd Scottish term, as such beer is dark in colour). Draught Wee Heavy, otherwise known as 90 Shilling or just Strong Ale, is Scotland's answer to barley wine, although it is a dark ale. It is claimed at the Belhaven brewery at Dunbar in East Lothian that people who drink it have been known afterwards to have thought they had met the ghost of a monk who used to brew in these parts a few centuries back. So beware!

The Scottish beer names 60/-, 70/- and 80/- are also used by Caley and Maclay's among others. Corresponding loosely to Mild, Bitter and Best Bitter respectively, beers with such designations can also be called Light, Special and Export (either of the latter sometimes being Heavy, a name now less used than in the past). The Shilling designations are reminders of the price of a barrel in Victorian times and are a rough guide to rising strength.

CAMRA has tried to make sure brewers only used the Shilling names for cask-conditioned beers, but some beers of this kind can be keg. Indeed Tennent's, the only Scottish brewing company to make no real ale of its own, uses 80/- as the title of a brewery-conditioned ale which used to be produced at the Heriot Brewery in Edinburgh, but which is being switched to the Wellpark Brewery in Glasgow – noted for lager since 1885 – with the closure of Heriot in the last half of 1992.

Tennent's used to make a cask version of 80/- at Heriot, but prefers to sell other people's real ale instead of making their own. Draught Bass – long absent from Scotland – has made a welcome return through the auspices of Tennent's, the Scottish subsidiary of Bass. Independent Scottish brewers can also sell their cask ales through Tennent's outlets.

The former chief executive of Tennent's, Mr Evelyn Matthews, has been responsible for a restructuring of the ownership of Maclay's of Alloa to give it a secure future. Since he acquired his interest in Maclay's, the company has started to expand its outlets for real ale. A nice change for the man once responsible for Scotland's biggest lager brewer! Maclay's ales have greatly improved recently. As well as 60/-, 70/- and 80/- and the great new Kane's Amber, another ale has recently been added to the Maclay range – Scotch Ale, a potent draught which is less sweet than when first test-marketed.

Alloa – where George Younger's famous brewery closed in 1963 – is home to the plant of the Alloa Brewery Company. All-lager for some years, its ale range now includes Archibald Arrol's Eighty Shilling, a pleasant cask brew. Alloa sells many guest ales, including Tetley Bitter and Burton Ale from its English associates.

The biggest brewery company headquartered in Scotland is Scottish & Newcastle, whose Edinburgh-brewed McEwan's 80/- was probably the most widely-available cask beer when CAMRA got started in Scotland. S&N faces a lot more competition on the cask front now, and is bringing Newcastle-brewed Theakstons to Scotland.

But if the survival of existing cask producers and the restoration of cask beer by others who had previously stopped making it adds up to success for CAMRA in Scotland, perhaps it is an even bigger accolade that new breweries have opened solely to meet demand for real ale in a country which almost lost it before CAMRA came along.

The oldest of the new breweries is Broughton in the Borders, where a £200,000 expansion project was formally declared open by George Younger, the former Cabinet Minister and descendant of the Alloa brewing family. His cousin David Younger is the managing director at Broughton, where Greenmantle Ale was introduced in 1980 and has been followed by others including Scottish Oatmeal Stout.

At Dollar, not far from Alloa, another new brewery has recently increased its output. This is Harviestoun, run by a former Ford area manager, Ken Brooker, whose range of real ales has a highly-appreciative audience. Another of the new generation of brewing companies to win widespread applause from Scottish ale lovers is managing to send such joys as Dark Island, Raven, and the mighty Skullsplitter all over the mainland from Britain's most northerly ale producer, the Orkney Brewery.

Smaller new breweries are Borve House at Ruthven, Aberdeenshire, and West Highland, on the historic Taynuilt station on the line to Oban. Even Traquair House, the oldest continuously-inhabited house in Scotland, has benefited from the real ale boom. Brewing of an ancient bottled ale was revived by the laird in 1965. Thanks to the draught enthusiasm inspired by CAMRA, cask-conditioned beers are also produced in the centuries-old brewhouse.

Most real ale in Scotland is dispensed by handpump, although traditionally the Scottish draught beer system used air pressure. Only a minority of pubs have kept the old equipment going, although some have been able to obtain modern versions of the tall founts (pronounced as though the "u" is missing) which allow the customer to see each pint being poured in full view. CAMRA does not accept carbon-dioxide or nitrogen pressure systems, but the Scottish air dispense is acceptable because of its tradition and because the beer comes out with a nice head, just as it might in Yorkshire when pulled through a tight sparkler. There is nothing "unreal" about ale dispensed in the Scottish way, but visitors who are uncertain when they see a tall metal column on the bar should ask if the beer is cask or not.

Whether in Aberdeen, Inverness, Dundee, Glasgow, Edinburgh, or many other parts of Scotland, real ale is again to be found in good condition in countless numbers of pubs. Scottish cask beer sales rose by 18 per cent in 1991, while keg ale and stout went into decline by 4.5 per cent. CAMRA supporters can take great pride in that achievement, coming after years of steady progress.

The signs are good for cask beer in Scotland, with more new and revived ales promised and further growth a certainty. Without CAMRA, it would all have been so different.

Allan McLean

THE GROWTH OF THE MICRO-BREWERIES

O F ALL CAMRA's achievement's, perhaps the least expected was the sudden appearance of a host of small breweries producing real ale. What began as a trickle in the mid-1970s became a flood of fresh firms by the end of the decade, pouring new life into a contracting industry.

For well over a century the number of breweries in Britain had been steadily declining as a few large combines came to dominate what was seen as a closed industry. No new brewing company had appeared for fifty years by the time the new wave rolled its first barrel against the mighty walls of monopoly power. As in most revolutions, the casualty rate was high. Many of the brave ventures quickly discovered that their beers were barred from more pubs than they had expected, either through the tied house system or by cheap loans from the big brewers. As one door was slammed in their faces another was bolted tight against them. In the small amount of genuine free trade, competition was fierce, slow payment was the rule and bad debts were rife. Despair, bankruptcy and closure followed.

But others struggled and survived to establish their names and beers in the local free trade, and even buy their own pubs. So far out of some 300 pint-sized pioneers almost half remain. And every year a handful more appear to widen our choice at the bar. This remarkable revolution has not been confined to Britain. Its infectious enthusiasm has spread around the globe from the US and Canada to New Zealand and Australia, often using British experience, expertise and equipment. But the roots of the revolt lie in CAMRA.

First draughts

Looking back, it seems inevitable that once the Campaign had stirred the public bar and made beer news again, some enthusiasts would put their money where their mouths were – or rather where they believed drinkers' mouths should be. Not surprisingly, the first bold pioneer was also a member of the original CAMRA National Executive.

'I foresaw the revival of interest in real ale, and got in early,' said Martin Sykes, who launched Selby Brewery in 1972. But his Yorkshire company was not a completely new concern. He had resurrected a family business dating back to 1894 which had ceased brewing in 1954, cleaning up the old vessels to start mashing again. Although the brewery never captured much of the local market and today is mainly a wholesale operation, Selby did capture many other people's imagination. His was the first barrel which set the rest rolling.

Two tinier ventures followed: the Miners Arms, Priddy, Somerset, in 1973, and the Masons Arms, South Leigh, Oxfordshire, the following year. They breathed life into the almost forgotten craft of the home-brew house, which by then was in serious danger of extinction. Only four pubs – the All Nations and the Three Tuns in Shropshire, the Old Swan in the West Midlands and the Blue Anchor in Cornwall – were still soldiering on brewing their own beer. Customers were fascinated, even though the Miners Arms was only a restaurant offering bottled beer. 'I've no intention of becoming a larger commercial brewery,' said owner Paul Leyton. 'I'm doing it for the sparkle on my customers' faces.'

The honour of stepping across the pub threshold and successfully selling into the fierce free trade goes to a professional brewer rejected by CAMRA's arch-enemy, Watney's. When Bill Urquart was dumped on the dole at the age of fifty-eight, after forty years in brewing, he bounced right back with his own Litchborough Brewery in 1974, set up in a barn next to his country home. It was while carrying out the soul-destroying task of running down Watney's Northampton Brewery, so it could be demolished to make way for the new Carlsberg plant, that he made the calculations which showed that small-scale brewing could make a profit – and good beer. He enjoyed the challenge of taking the battle to the giants. 'Brewers have been edged aside in favour of people who talk about economics rather than beer. Everyone now has to be trained in the concept of marginal profits. They've swamped out the people who want to make good beer. Once the head brewers used to decide what the beer would be. Now they make what they are told.' He had planned to brew a few gallons and play a lot of golf. But his Northamptonshire Bitter proved too popular. Even his golf club sold it. 'It's fifteen hours a day, seven days a week. I'm working twice as hard as I did before.'

Soon not just thirsty customers were flocking to his door. Other pint-size pioneers – Peter Austin of Ringwood Brewery, Nigel Fitzhugh of Blackawton, Simon Whitmore of Butcombe – came as well to see how it was done. Six fresh ventures appeared in 1977, with seven the following year. The revolution had begun.

The brewers

The new brewers came from all walks of life. Some were devoted real ale drinkers and CAMRA members like Victoria Brewery in Hertfordshire and Leith in Edinburgh. Bourne Valley in Hampshire was established by a former CAMRA national chairman, James Lynch. Others were experienced brewery executives who had tired of working for others and decided to strike out on their own. Simon Whitmore left his prestigious post as managing director of Courage Western to set up his Butcombe Brewery in Avon in 1978; in the same year David Younger of the celebrated Scottish brewing family founded his own Broughton Brewery in the Scottish Borders.

Crucially, a small number of experienced brewers began to act as consultants, providing both the equipment and the expertise to allow others to become brewers. Peter Austin, former head brewer of Hull Brewery, not only established his own Ringwood Brewery but spawned many more from Archers and Ballards to Woods. In ten years he helped set up over forty breweries. Peter Shardlow, group production director, and Robin Richards took early retirement from Whitbread to form Inn Brewing in 1982. In their first year alone, they installed ten breweries.

Some of these new ventures were extensions of existing businesses, many being established by enterprising pub landlords, first to serve their own bar and then others. Clarks of Wakefield and Powells of Central Wales were major beer wholesalers. Moles of Wiltshire and the New Forest Brewery were soft drinks companies. Stocks of Doncaster rose out of a bakery business. Some were very small; a few being born in off-licences, like Pitfield of London. John Payne's Smiles Brewery in Bristol started brewing in a restaurant before his cheeky grin widened into a business jolly enough to worry the big brewers.

Others began on a grander scale. Tisbury Brewery of Wiltshire was launched on the stock market in a blaze of publicity and a shower of shares to become the industry's answer to 'Dallas,' with enough boardroom battles, merger talks, financial scandals and takeovers to sustain a major TV series. Eventually Tisbury ran four breweries across the South of England, before this mini-empire collapsed in a storm of recriminations and debt.

By the early 1980s the trickle had become a flood. Sixteen new breweries came on stream in 1979, eighteen in 1980, thirty-six in 1981, thirty-two in 1982...the movement was so successful even the big brewers jumped on the small beer waggon. Whitbread set up eleven home-brew pubs, Watney's seven, Allied twelve.

The national companies were particularly impressed by the punning performance of David Bruce. From the Goose & Firkin in Southwark in 1979, he had unleashed a chain of high profile home-brew pubs in London, each with their own Firkin flavour of bare boards and horrendous humour. By the time he sold his twelve houses in 1988, the bustling business was worth £6.6 million.

The problems

But for each success story there was a sorrier saga. Home-brew pubs were the safest option as they provided a reliable outlet for the beers as well as the retail profit. New brewers who relied solely on the free trade, without any houses of their own, were on more dangerous ground. They might brew the best beers in Britain – some of them did according to CAMRA's competitions – but they lacked the financial muscle to keep their ales on the bar when representatives of the big brewers barged in waving their cheque books and offering cheap loans. They could only counter this with flexible, local service and quality products.

The success rate varied from area to area, depending on regional conditions. The South-west of England proved a good breeding ground because of its widespread free trade; the North-west, in Lancashire, proved difficult because of its lack of genuine free houses. Areas dominated by major brewers were worst of all. In Wales, out of eighteen bold ventures only two still survive.

The tied houses were the first barrier, closing many pubs to the new beers. Ian Hornsey, of the Nethergate Brewery in Suffolk, stated in 1988: 'The tied-house system means that, in our area, eighty per cent of the market is closed to us.' But it is the insidious financial inducements in the remaining free trade that really angers the new brewers. 'It is all very wrong', said Peter Austin of Ringwood. 'These sort of loans are illegal in America and Germany, and it's about time something was done about them here.'

They are a particular problem in the West Country where many free houses are bought and sold every year. 'We nearly always lose customers when the pub changes hands because of these loans,' said Nigel Fitzhugh of Blackawton Brewery in Devon.

In the North the position is worse. Terry Hanson of Big Lamp Brewery in Newcastle said free trade on Tyneside 'is virtually non-existent due to large brewery loans.' Michael Jenkinson, of Stocks Brewery in Doncaster, added: 'If legislation were passed to outlaw the cheap big loan policies of the larger established breweries, then the small brewer would have a chance to secure accounts in the free trade, purely on the merit of his product and the devotion most put into making it.'

Some customers do not help by delaying payment for beer supplied. Bad debts are a constant problem, especially since the brewer has to pay for his materials and the heavy excise duty long before his payment comes in. Tony Burns of the Victoria Brewery in Hertfordshire, which closed in 1985, recalled: 'Our biggest problem was getting paid. We could have been profitable on twenty barrels a week, if we could have collected our money promptly. The difficulty was that you wanted to retain the outlet as well as get your money. We needed the outlets too badly, as we had no pubs of our own to fall back on. But we could not afford to buy pubs as we did not have enough capital to start with.'

Some solutions

To help fight their corner, the new brewers formed their own Small Independent Brewers Association (SIBA) in 1980. They had little choice. The existing Brewers' Society, which represents the vested interests of the major brewers, had refused to accept the new brewers as members, since they knew that their aims were in conflict. The Government was also concerned about the state of the industry and instructed the Monopolies and Mergers Commission to investigate the supply of beer in the UK. The radical proposals published in 1989, after threatening to ban restrictive loans, were well watered down. But some houses are to be freed from the tie and tenants of the major brewers were given the right to stock a guest real ale of their choice from May 1990.

This should have opened up a whole new market for the new brewers. But most tenants have been slow to experiment, worried by threatened rent rises by their brewers. Many of the nationals have also supplied their own preferred lists of guest beers, with the implication that tenants who stray from the list could run into problems.

'There is still an element of doubt in many large brewery licensees' minds as to their right to buy a guest beer from an independent supplier,' reported Peter Mauldon of Mauldon's Brewery in Sudbury, Suffolk.

Some of the new brewers like Burton Bridge in Burton-on-Trent began to wholesale other new brewers' beers so they could offer a wider range of guest ales. In areas like the south-west, members of SIBA even banded together in co-operative ventures to swap beers. The market was disappointingly sluggish at first, but then began to pick up.

'Five per cent of our outlets are now tied houses,' says Carola Brown of

Ballards Brewery in Hampshire. 'It was very slow to start with, but it is taking off now.' Archers of Swindon reported a ten per cent increase in business. Simon Whitmore of Butcombe Brewery in Avon was enthusiastic. 'We have profited appreciably from the guest ale clause; so much so that we are thinking of enlarging the brewery.'

But will this guest beer market in the big brewers' tied houses last? Some doubt it. 'The Big Five will soon out-smart the M&MC Report and the guest beer in tied pubs will die,' believes Rob Viney of the Ash Vine Brewery in Somerset. Ray Ashworth of Woodforde's Norfolk Ales says that in the first year of the guest beer market from May 1990, his sales increased by thirty-five per cent thanks to new business in the tied trade. But since then, the nationals have been hitting back with somewhat underhand tactics by giving cash discounts 'in excess of our own gross profit margin!' David Roberts of the Pilgrim Brewery in Surrey foresaw 'the possible loss of the guest beer market as a result of the majors dumping beer into it'.

Most agree there is one major way that the Government could redress the balance, and give David a chance in his battle against the Goliaths of the industry. Denis Armstrong of the new Hull Brewery spelt it out: 'The implementation of a sliding scale of excise duty would give smaller breweries a better chance of competing with the majors in the market place.' In Germany such a sliding scale, where small breweries pay less duty, has helped preserve many of the country's traditional family firms.

Others would like to see positive action on the constant problem of slow payment. Ray Ashworth of Woodforde's would like the Government to 'overhaul drastically our credit laws and debt recovery procedures' by introducing 'a system akin to German law where credit is limited to two weeks with penalties imposed for default'.

The recession is biting hard and many report an increase in the number of pubs going out of business. Simon Whitmore of Butcombe says he had more bad debts in 1991 than in the whole of the previous twelve years. Big firms can absorb losses that can cripple smaller concerns. Most want to see a more vigorous monitoring and enforcement of the M&MC recommendations and the introduction if possible of the original proposals. Chains of pubs over the 2,000 mark should be included in the guest ale ruling. In Scotland, new brewers are particularly incensed that Scottish & Newcastle Breweries have been allowed to sidestep the regulations by reducing their number of pubs below the 2,000 mark.

Some want tenants of all breweries, irrespective of size, to be allowed to stock a guest ale. This is not just selfish pleading, as most of the new brewers happily stock guest beers in their own pubs. They know variety increases business.

'I believe the greatest effect of the M&MC Report has been the way the publicity surrounding it has drawn attention to traditional beers generally,' says Jennifer Aries of the Cotleigh Brewery in Somerset. 'As a result of the report, the industry has spent a fortune on advertising traditional beers. The drinking public are now thinking and talking about real ale – they have become much more aware of all the different types of traditional beer and are enjoying them. The traditional beer market is enjoying enormous growth in both the free and tied trade.'

The achievements

Given the 'closed shop' in which the new brewers have tried to sell their beer, it is remarkable that so many have survived and succeeded. CAMRA's 1991 *Good Beer Guide* detailed ninety-four new free trade brewers, from the Paradise Brewery in Hayle, Cornwall, to the Orkney Brewery, plus forty-two new home-brew pubs. Less than twenty years ago, none of these existed. Their arrival and survival is a major achievement in itself. They might be tiny, no more than a few grains in the nation's mash tun, accounting in total for less than one per cent of the beer brewed in Britain. But they have greatly increased the choice available for drinkers prepared to pass a few bars in search of new brews and virtually all brew only real ale.

And they have not only added welcome variety in terms of fresh bitters, they have also dared to pioneer the resurgence of some neglected beer styles. Porter, once a popular beer in Britain, has been revived by the enterprise of brewers like Burton Bridge in Burton-on-Trent, Oak in Cheshire and Mauldons of Suffolk. They have spearheaded the revival of strong draught ales, often with delightful names like Hobgoblin from Glenny Brewery in Oxfordshire, Topsy Turvy from Berrow in Somerset and Old Smokey from Bunces in Wiltshire. Some have increased the limited number of bottle-conditioned beers in Britain.

They have added a fresh draught of imagination at the bar, with a few of the latest ventures treading even more exotic ground. One, Packhorse Brewing in Kent, is producing traditional German beers, including a dark Munich-style lager.

Besides choice and local colour, the new brewers have also added that vital ingredient: quality. 'Our advantage is the quality of our product – we do not brew to a Big Six budget,' says Colin Bocking of Crouch Vale in Essex. Pitfield Brewery of London won the 1987 Champion Beer of Britain at CAMRA's Great British Beer Festival with their rare old ale, Dark Star. Golden Hill of Somerset can boast the distinction of winning the bitter award in the same contest in 1980, within weeks of starting production.

Above all, in an era of growing demand for natural products, almost all the new ventures brew only from traditional ingredients, using a high proportion of malted barley and whole hops. They have no need for the chemical preservatives and head-foaming agents used by the giants in their processed beer factories. They have made brewing a craft again rather than an industry. Significantly, when CAMRA campaigned for beer to join other foodstuffs in listing ingredients, the new brewers had no objection and, indeed, led the way in providing drinkers with details of what goes into their pint. In contrast, the major brewers shuffled with embarrassment, evaded the issue, and eventually refused to name their ingredients in a cloud of lame excuses. One is left wondering what they have got to hide.

The new boys also have much to offer licensees. As the giants grow ever bigger and more remote from the local pub, so the small brewer can fill the gap by providing a more personal service. The man who drives the dray may also be the brewer; so the landlord can talk straight to the chap in charge. If a pub runs out of beer at the weekend, only the new brewers have the flexibility – and concern – to deliver. They can even produce a special 'house' beer for individual outlets.

Edward Wood of Woods Brewery in Shropshire attacks the high-pricing policies of the major brewers, with their regular annual rises, often well above inflation. He has refused to follow their lead in jacking up the price of a pint. He said, 'There is little justification for such price increases other than to pump up profits as a hedge against falling beer sales. We are only minnows in the brewery ocean, but maybe we can play a small part in trying to break the vicious circle of beer price increases that is driving pub customers to the supermarkets and drinking at home.'

The pint-size progress has since the mid-Eighties steadied in Britain, with only a few new breweries now appearing each year as others close down. Yet the revolution is far from over. Instead it has spread around the world, thanks to the efforts of consultants like Peter Austin. After helping establish breweries in England and Wales, it was one hop to Hilden Brewery in Belfast and then another across the Atlantic to Newman's Brewery in New York state, sparking the revolution in North America. By 1987 the number of new breweries there had exploded to seventy-five. Schemes followed in Germany, France and Belgium. By the late Eighties, Peter Austin was working one month building a plant in Nigeria and the next setting up small communal breweries in China.

Inn Brewing also went globe trotting, from the Palo Alto Brewing Company in San Francisco to the Ballarat Brewery in Australia, the first new brewery down under. Peter Shardlow and Robin Richards established Italy's first brewpub in Sorrento and built one in Bavaria for Prince Luitpold von Bayern. They ventured beyond the iron curtain in 1985, into Hungary, and also reached Canada, New Zealand and the West Indies.

What had begun as a few far-fetched plans in Britain had captured the imagination of the world.

Brian Glover

REAL FOOD AT THE INN

CAMRA MEMBERS WILL know and love the famous Fleece at Bretforton, a jewel in the crown of the National Trust. I can remember visiting the Fleece well before the NT took over – indeed, before it was briefly a CAMRA Real Ale Investments house. Jointly run by two elderly landladies of fluttering charm and courtesy who hung the times of the church services on the door, they passed you a pint straight from the barrel as if handing the vicar a cup of tea.

On my first visit I was feeling peckish and asked if they did sandwiches. Regretfully, no. Perhaps a bag of crisps, then? More in sorrow than in anger one of the 'Miss Marples' leaned towards me and whispered in slightly shocked tones, 'My dear, this is a *pub.*'

It's an attitude I have met several times; CAMRA members themselves have occasionally expressed it. And editor of *Good Pub Food* as I am, I have sometimes felt a sneaking sympathy with the concept of a good old-fashioned boozer; no frills, no flowers, no carpets, not a pickled egg in sight – just sawdust on the floor and superb real ales cared for by a cellarman obsessed with his calling. Then I remind myself that this may be the traditional image of the pub, but it's a relatively recent tradition. OK, when CAMRA was launched twenty-one years ago precious few pubs offered meals, but that's relatively modern history.

I prefer to take my image of the perfect pub from a far earlier rôle model, the inn that succoured weary travellers, and happily there is no shortage of examples from days of yore. Did Chaucer's worldy pilgrims stop off at Le Manoir aux Quat' Saisons or the Little Chef? No, their leisurely journey to Canterbury had them bedding down at some splendid highway hostelries where they passed the evening in convivial feasting and tale telling. There are evocative descriptions of pub food, veritable banquets in some cases, in the writing of previous centuries from Pepys to Pickwick. Even at Daphne du Maurier's sinister Jamaica Inn you could expect a decent repast.

At some point relatively recently, it simply ceased to be. Pubs either served no food at all – 'What do you think this is? A fish and chip shop?' – or worse still insulted our stomachs with gruesome comestibles that became the butt of the stand-up comedian: ghastly rolls mouldering under plastic domes; jumbo sausages; gristly pasties; individual pork pies served, just as they reached the pub, in cellophane. What Keith Floyd eloquently described in his foreword to my first guide when he talked about pub food as 'an horrific phrase that all too often refers to plates of badly prepared, factory-made pizzas, chilli or lasagne, piled high with artificially coloured coleslaw and a microwaved jacket potato .... Or even (perhaps) worse, processed rectangles of "cheese", bad bread and a pale onion preserved in acetic acid offered as a ploughperson's lunch. Ugh'.

For too long, the myth survived the reality. I don't say that examples of the above are no longer found; sadly, there is still some vile pub grub masquerading as food. (Fortunately, I seldom have to eat it because CAMRA members put me in the way of some brilliant pub lunches.) But the joke has grown rather stale, while the food itself has got fresher and fresher.

As recently as 1988, when I was researching the first *Pub Food*, pubs were still regarded as the twilight zone of catering. Restaurant critics and food writers alike were airily dismissive, including the present incumbent at *The Good Food Guide* who has since become more warmly disposed. In short, a distinctly snobbish attitude prevailed from those who moved in the world of Michelin stars. Genuine foodies wouldn't be seen dead eating in a pub.

Perhaps it took the recession to prove it, as even the well-heeled baulked at restaurant prices, but even then a revolution was taking place in pub eats, and the pace of change has accelerated over the past two years. My claim when the first guide appeared that good British pubs were fast catching up with French auberges on the food front, sparking some controversy at the time, barely raises an eyebrow now.

In setting out our stall as Real Ale and Real Food, we certainly touched a nerve. What's more, I believe we have done much to bring good pub cooks the recognition they deserve. They have certainly been keen to talk to me about their different styles of cooking, and even share their recipes.

Some pubs even produce the ingredients they use in their cooking, like the one with a dairy making Caerphilly. A few with their own smokeries smoke both meat and fish; many publicans grow vegetables (prize-winning in one case I recall) and herbs; I found a pub keeping goats to turn their milk into both yoghurt and cheese; some with free-range hens providing eggs for cooking; a pub where the bee-keeping landlord made honey, even one with its own herd of pedigree cattle.

One of the great joys has been discovering so many pub cooks using the regional produce of their area and preserving traditional local dishes – often handed down through their families – that might otherwise be lost to use for good. In the past year I've visited a Welsh landlord who goes down to his local beach to gather laverbread, then fries it with cockles on a stove fuelled by driftwood. He told me: 'It looks exactly like a black ribbon that you'd tie in your hair. You've got to wash it several times because if you leave even one bit of grit or barnacle in it, that's one bit too many. In west Wales they cook it in a cauldron and it comes out rather sloppy – I do it like my grandmother used to, baked in the oven with strips of bacon.'

At a pub in Cumbria I tasted for the first time Cumbrian Tatie Ash, a thick lamb and beef stew traditionally topped with pickled beetroot. This was served at a pub in fell-walking country where the lamb and beef is reared on the licensees' own farm.

Not many miles away is a pub where Cumbria, Lancashire and Yorkshire meet and you can eat Lakeland Pie of bacon, apple and sage, Cumberland sausage with home-made chutney, and Westmorland Cottage Pie flavoured with black pudding.

Crossing towards the Scarborough coast you come to one of my very favourite pubs hidden in the Yorkshire Wolds, where the landlady offers jugged hare, pies of rabbit in brown ale, pot-roasted pheasants and savoury sage pudding. Stay the night and there is porridge before the fry-up, home-made marmalade afterwards.

Then there's the real ale bar above a high-class butcher's and grocer's in

Edinburgh making its own haggis and boiling tripe in a vast cellar catacomb. Both are sold in the bar along with home-potted hough, soda bread, Highland lamb stew with barley and superb roast Scottish beef.

Coming South, I've visited the Midlands pub whose landlady helped set up the Black Country Museum and delights regulars with recipes from their book *Bostin Fittle* – gray payes and bacon, grorty dick, boiled ham with parsley sauce and real faggots wrapped in the pig's caul. Round the other side of Birmingham is the pub smoking its own kippers in the Mad O'Rourke chain.

In Norfolk I've eaten crab at an inn where the cook brings them fresh from her family's fishing boat, in Kent enjoyed Kentish lamb pie flavoured with apples, sultanas and chutney, and in Avon a Yokel's Pudding of apples and cider served with thick, organic cream.

Truth to tell, during the past few years writing the guides and features for *What's Brewing*, I've been converted myself. Eating in posh restaurants no longer has the same appeal. Quite recently I was sitting in one of Kensington's finest, toying with something pretty on a plate and sipping a frighteningly expensive wine, when I thought 'I wish I was eating Barry's Sussex Bacon Pudding washed down with a pint of Ballards!'

Talking of beer with food, I believe that is one of the exciting developments still to come. Just a few publicans have started creating beer lists in the style of wine lists, showing that there is a whole range of different styles of ale to complement different foods. Over the next few years, I hope there will be many more. Lots of pubs, of course, use their real ale as an ingredient, like the landlord who mixes it into his bread dough and several who use it as a lightening agent in both Yorkshire pudding and fish batter. Cheese and ale soup is delicious, so is Guinness fruit cake, and two of the best pies I've ever tasted are cooked at a pub near Hadrian's Wall – the boozer's pie based on a recipe first devised by monks on Holy Island of beef marinated in stout and cider with spinach, and steak braised in Old Peculier with onions, honey and asparagus tips.

It would be wrong to give the impression that all pubs are concentrating on British cookery. We now have landlords and landladies of many ethnic backgrounds creating a diverse range of cuisines from Chinese to Malaysian. The only real prawn crackers I have ever eaten were in a pub, and I've also tasted Thai, Sri Lankan, regional Indian, Portuguese, Yugoslavian, Mexican, Cajun and even Peruvian.

Real-ale-quaffing vegetarians would probably agree that they are better catered for in pubs than they used to be. Even so, there are still far too many vegetable lasagnes around and even – quite unforgivable – ignorant publicans who list fish dishes on the vegetarian menu. But I've also seen eighteenth century Gloucester Pie, described as one of the original vegetarian dishes; Israeli chick pea balls; stir-fry tofu with peanuts; broccoli and mushroom pie; chestnut burger and plenty of pasta with fresh herb sauces.

Another encouraging development is the number of good young chefs who are choosing to take on a pub rather than a restaurant, bringing a whole new dimension of original and creative cooking to the pub scene. As one said to me: 'There is great scope for family-run pubs in this country – having a drinks and snacks trade as well as the meals side makes the whole operation so much more viable.'

There is, of course, no room for complacency in pub food as in any other area of the brewing industry or licensed trade. Beware the onward march of the theme pub with designer-led menus, and portion-controlled centrally produced frozen or quick-chill dishes – the antithesis of real food freshly prepared by real cooks.

As for concerning ourselves with pub food, twenty-one years ago CAMRA obviously had to be single-minded. The task was to get real ale back into pubs. As that campaign was won, the aims naturally broadened to include the protection of the public house itself. It is right that CAMRA should concern itself with the pub as a whole, and that includes real food along with real cider, real bar games, real fires and real entertainment.

Susan Nowak

COMPETITION AND THE M&MC

THE UK BREWING industry has been the subject of numerous investigations over the last two decades. It remains to be proved that this activity has actually done the consumer any good.

Official reports on the industry have been critical, but until recently little has come in the way of Government action. The 1989 Monopolies and Mergers Commission Report did produce intervention in the name of widening consumer choice and increasing competition. However, the results have been far from satisfactory. Further probes by Whitehall and Brussels are inevitable.

Why has the brewing industry been so thoroughly investigated?

The majority of adults visit the pub at least once a month. People like their drink, and price rises are viewed with unusual hostility. CAMRA's phone never stops ringing for the couple of days after the brewers put up prices. For the last decade or more, prices have risen faster than inflation, and the bigger companies are significantly more expensive than the independent brewers.

The industry is a big employer, it makes big profits, and the Government takes an enormous rake from the price of a pint in tax. UK brewers are not large in European terms, but they are high in the profit ranks of European brewers.

Pubs, and local breweries, are part of local communities, and inspire passions in the way few other industries can. Alcohol is seen by many as a dangerous drug. The Government has interfered in its sale for centuries, not least through a licensing system which allows local magistrates to judge whether there is 'need' for new outlets.

Finally, the industry has an unusual structure, which attracts the hostility of many competition policy theorists. If there is such a thing as a 'normal' pattern of competition, manufacturers and retailers are usually separate companies.

In 1989, British brewers owned over half of the country's pubs, and over sixty per cent of beer was sold through tied houses. The theorists call this 'vertical integration'. They believe that it allows the manufacturer to dominate the retailer, to the detriment of the consumer. This academic line of thinking makes officialdom hostile to the industry.

Taking these points together, it isn't surprising that the UK brewing industry has been the object of constant political surveillance.

The price isn't right

It is probably the price issue which most concerns the powers that be. There is something in the pub-goers' blood which makes them resent paying for their pleasure. Supping a pint of Bass, after yet another price rise, Joe Public learns that the Chairman of Bass has had a 45 per cent pay rise, and can put two and two together.

Certainly the brewing industry has its own logic in price terms. There are usually two price rises a year, whether the Chancellor raises taxes or not.

There is serious over-capacity in the industry. Brewers could produce 50 million barrels of beer a year, but we only drink 36 million. In many industries, that would have triggered a price cutting war to win market share. Not so in the pub, where beer prices rise faster than inflation. It is a strange sort of business where supply exceeds demand, where demand is declining, and yet prices are not dented.

Takeovers and concentration
The story of the "Big Six" has often been told. During the Fifties and the Sixties, big was beautiful. Hundreds of independent brewers disappeared into the maw of the conglomerates, six national combines who closed scores of breweries and axed hundreds of brands.

Whitbread also established a sinister network of 'defensive' shareholdings in other companies, called the "Whitbread umbrella". The price for qualified independence was a Whitbread man on your board, and Whitbread beers in your pubs.

The 1969 Monopolies Commission report was a shot across the big brewers' bows. Allied's bid for Boddingtons was defeated, and hostile bids went out of fashion, at least until S&N went shopping for their competitors in the Eighties. However, the national brewers continued their growth by other means.

True, brewers sold pubs. The proportion of pubs owned outright by brewers declined between 1969 and 1989. However, most of the pubs they sold, or closed, were small-volume outlets. The nationals' market share continued to grow. Those pubs which were sold as free houses were often tied with loans, ensuring guaranteed outlets for the big brewers' beers.

National advertising built national brands, paid for by higher prices in the brewers' enormous tied estates. The keg bitter revolution failed to sweep all before it, but lager was more successful. Millions of pounds a year, over twenty years, successfully created a growing market for a weak and over-priced product that no German would be seen dead drinking. Local brewers had to follow the national trend.

Nor were we free from takeovers and mergers. National brewers could spot a bargain. Ruddles sold out to Grand Metropolitan; S&N acquired Theakstons, Matthew Brown, and Home; Whitbread bought Boddingtons, and Allied now brew for Greenall Whitley. Many of the famous names from the Seventies are now in the national brewers' pockets.

Regional brewers tried to reach national scale. Greenalls devoured Simpkiss and Davenports, and destroyed old acquisitions Shipstones and Wem as well. Boddingtons took over Higsons and Oldham, before leaving brewing. A new round of regional mergers seems likely in the Nineties, triggered by the 1991 bid by Boddingtons for Devenish.

This march of concentration has seen a steady stream of brewery closures, and the disappearance of well-loved local beers. Customers have less choice, and higher prices to pay for more unwieldy companies.

Pubs too have suffered, with the accountants closing down smaller "uneconomic" outlets. Crass retailing concepts have spread from head office downwards, removing individuality from tied estates.

Finally, even the "Big Six" felt insecure and wanted to get bigger. Under Australian ownership, Courage tried to take over Allied, then to take over S&N. They were blocked by the Monopolies and Mergers Commission. Finally they settled for marriage with Grand Metropolitan, of which more later.

The analysts would be happy to see Allied leave brewing, and the likely purchasers of its breweries would further concentrate ownership in the hands of the majors.

This concentration of power in the industry disturbs the public, and is a major reason for CAMRA's recent leap in membership.

Questioning the tie

Since investigations into the industry invariably start by questioning the tied house system, we should ask how strong the case against it is.

International comparisons are tricky. However, the three EC countries with the most diverse beer markets are those where the tied house is most prevalent – Germany, Belgium and the UK.

On the other hand, a single brewer dominates countries such as Denmark, Ireland, Holland and America, where the tie has been banned or is not significant. Two companies have over ninety per cent of the Australian market, where the tie has been abolished.

There seems little serious doubt that the tied house system preserves independent breweries. Local brewers can establish a presence and a local indentity through the pubs they own. The tied house allows small producers, trading within a controlled area, to be competitive in price terms against the nationals.

Were we to abolish the tie in the UK, few independent brewers would survive against a flood of nationally advertised brands.

The majority of pubs would probably pass into the hands of enormous retailers. If this happened, like the supermarkets, they would demand massive discounts from their suppliers, and only the largest and most ruthless producers could meet their demands.

Given the choice, most family brewers would have to choose to keep their pubs, not their breweries. Of course some would stay in brewing, but they would become niche producers, charging above the odds for better beer. They would become the equivalent of delicatessens or boutiques, catering to a tiny minority of customers.

Unlike most modern markets, there is great diversity in beer, and the tastiest products cost no more than the bland and mass-produced. That diversity would be sacrificed if the tie were to be abolished.

Certainly, the scale of the tied house system in the UK protects the national brewers against a degree of price competition. The tie has, up until now, been more prevalent in the UK than elsewhere; the on-trade more important than elsewhere; and the industry more concentrated than Germany, where there are more than a thousand brewers. To highlight the tie's good features is not to give the industry a clean bill of health.

But every time the European Commission has looked at the tied house, they have started off wanting to abolish it, and ended up keeping it. While the matter will once again be examined in 1997, and any decision is possible, it is difficult to escape the belief that the tie benefits consumers, by giving them something worth drinking, and it should be retained.

The march of competition policy

The 1969 Monopolies Commission investigation into the industry could be taken as typical of most competition investigations. It was critical, the industry refused to accept its findings, and the Government ignored its recommendations.

The 1969 M&MC considered the issue of whether the consumer preferred a diverse beer market. They decided that the tie restricted competition, but considered it impossible to do anything about it. They placed their faith in reform of the licensing system.

Doubtless looser licensing would encourage local competition. A notoriously conservative licensing bench in Birmingham has entrenched the local Ansells/M&B duopoly by preventing competitors from opening pubs.

However, a flood of new licences would not alter the domination of the market by the national brewers. They would have the muscle to open many of the new outlets themselves, and they would tie up supposedly free outlets through the use of low-interest loans. The national brewers' marketing power would not be diminished.

A flood of new outlets might lower standards, but when the dust settled, we would find pretty much the same companies in charge, competing (or not) very much as they do now.

It proved to be an academic argument. The 1969 report, and the 1973 Erroll report (which reached the same conclusions as the M&MC for different reasons) were both ignored.

The 1977 Prices Commission report said that restrictive licensing, vertical integration and limited imports, taken together, protected the brewers against competition. Indeed they said that these were 'the classic conditions for a monopoly, acting against the consumer interest'.

The Commission found that national brewers charged more for their beer than the local brewers – something which a decade of CAMRA price surveys continues to find. However, the national brewers did not make higher profits. Their higher costs were swallowed up in top-heavy management, advertising, higher distribution costs and the like. The consumer gained no benefit from the concentration of smaller brewers into larger.

But the Prices Commission made no recommendations. The Government of the day came up with a cosmetic proposal which was rightly mocked: pub swaps. Every national brewer agreed to try to reduce the number of pubs they owned in the licensing districts where they had more than half the pubs. In fact only three larger licensing districts were covered! The pubs were usually swapped with other nationals. Limited as the programme of pub swaps was, it was not fully monitored and was never completed.

Clearly it marginally improved competition to open a few Courage pubs in Norfolk (dominated by Watney's) and to open a few Watney's pubs in Bristol (dominated by Courage). But it amounted to re-arranging the deckchairs, not changing the direction of the ship. Six companies continued to own (or otherwise tie) sufficient of the country's pubs to dominate the industry, and decide just how much competition they wanted.

The 1987-89 M&MC enquiry was different, because it produced action. The consequences of the report, and the Government's actions, show just how difficult it is to change the way an industry runs.

This M&MC panel started with three broad prejudices. They supported the smaller producers, who they thought got a bad deal. They supported the tenants, who they thought were treated badly. And as abstract competition policy theorists par excellence, they were hostile to the larger brewers' tied estates. They clearly liked the idea of 'normal' competition, with powerful retailers and independent wholesalers, acting to keep the producers of beer under control.

The M&MC Report recommended that no brewer be allowed to own more than two thousand pubs; that tieing free houses through loans should be banned; that tenants should be given legal security of tenure; that tenants should be free to stock the guest beer of their choice. The report was only advisory and it was for the Government to decide what (if any) action to take.

Even the M&MC's greatest fans would agree that the report was a strange document. At times it resembled an argument between two crusty professors of economics, each of whom hated the other and would not concede a single point.

The M&MC found there was a 'complex monopoly' in the industry – a term so loosely defined in the Fair Trading Act that it could be summarised as 'a situation where the M&MC does not like what it sees'.

The M&MC decided that all the profit in the big brewers' operation was in brewing beer. They decided that the brewers ran their tied estates at low profit levels to strangle price competition; hence the famous proposal to limit brewers to two thousand pubs each. The unkind might say that this discovery fitted rather conveniently with the academic prejudice that vertical integration amounts to producer domination of an industry.

However, within the industry itself, it is widely believe that running pubs is more profitable than brewing beer. Most breweries are underutilised. The Eighties was the decade of the retailer, when manufacturing was a dirty word. Pubs, with their food operations and amusement machines, offer much more exciting opportunities than the dreary business of brewing.

Faced with the choice posed by the M&MC, most national brewers would have either split into two nominally independent operations – Bass Pubs and Bass Breweries, say – or they would have sold their breweries to someone else. Not what the M&MC or the Government expected!

The M&MC also tried to have brewers' loans to free houses banned. But the loan tie is so widespread in Europe that it seems unlikely that the European Commission would ever let it be prohibited. Certainly the Government's U-turn on this was massive, although they did ensure that all loans could be paid off promptly and the tie ended.

What the Government ended up with was a compromise. The national brewers had to reduce the number of pubs they tied, under the curious 'free half the number over two thousand' rule.

Tenants were allowed to stock a guest beer. This was defined as a real ale, to the irritation of Guinness and the lager companies, and to the delight of CAMRA.

Tenants would be given security of tenure by 1992, giving the brewers plenty of time to get the tenants out beforehand, if they so wanted.

The effects of the Government's proposals would be reviewed by the Office of Fair Trading in 1993. And the European Commission announced that it too would mount a review, just to check that the UK's review had gone far enough – a review of the review, if you like – and that nothing had to be done before the 1997 European-wide review of the tied house system.

One might feel almost sympathetic for the UK brewers, facing another three investigations of their industry over the next decade.

What happened next

In many ways the M&MC became a boon for the major brewers. Suddenly they could close breweries and blame the M&MC. They could sack workers, and the unions would blame the M&MC, not the brewers. They could try to arrange bigger and better mergers, and say it had been forced on them by the M&MC. And of course they could carry on putting up prices.

For years the accountants had urged the brewers to put their tenants on to long leases, which allow the brewers to raise higher rents and shift the burden of repairing the pub onto the tenants. Now the M&MC became the excuse to sack tenants and replace them with managers; to force tenants to sign leases on massive rents or be evicted; to close small pubs, and all the other nasty things the brewers had felt a bit restrained about before.

Boddingtons decided to leave brewing before the M&MC reported. Yet their decision is still quoted as a *consequence* of the M&MC.

Scottish and Newcastle spent years deliberately running down Matthew Brown, by transferring brewing elsewhere, cutting promotion of its products, and introducing rival brands into its market area. S&N had to divest no more than 1% of their total production under the M&MC proposals. Yet when they decided to close Matthew Brown, they blamed the M&MC. Brent Walker over-borrowed and got into trouble with their bankers – but if the Camerons brewery is closed, it will be blamed on the M&MC.

Competition policy's finest hour must have been the decision to allow the Grand Metropolitan – Courage deal to go ahead. In 1989 the M&MC blocked Courage from bidding for S&N. In 1991, they decided to let Courage merge with Grand Metropolitan, who own three thousand pubs *more* than S&N. The logic of this decision is difficult to discern.

Courage bought Grand Metropolitan's breweries. Courage and Grand Metropolitan will merge their tenanted estates into one company, Inntrepeneur Estates, jointly owned. A supply deal between Courage and the pub company provides for a declining tie, so that in theory Inntrepeneur ends up free of a formal tie altogether.

Not only was the Secretary of State's decision inconsistent, it also clearly acted to reduce competition. It was a classic case of believing that the problem was the degree of vertical integration, not the size of the companies concerned.

Courage will not go after Bass, the market leader, who are still somewhat protected by their tied estate. It is the smaller companies who will face the onslaught of advertising, loans, and discounts. The wholesale beer market will become more restricted, not less. The prerequisite for any rational attempt to restructure the brewing industry would have been the prohibition of any such mergers.

Conclusions

It has not all been a litany of gloom. In some areas the guest beer has been successful, and some of the microbrewers in particular have seen big increases in sales. A genuine local need is being satisfied.

While most tenants who take guest beers do so from their breweries' approved lists, some do exercise their independence. In a couple of cases, breweries have reopened, to meet the perceived need for locally-brewed cask beers. The national companies are starting to see that the customer wants a wider choice, and are – in their own way – working towards accommodating that need.

Pub sales to smaller brewers have both saved those pubs from over-refurbishment, and have marginally diluted local monopolies. Independent brewers have significantly increased the size of their tied estates. Some of the new free house chains which have begun to appear do offer a genuine choice, although some threaten to be worse exploiters of their pubs than the breweries.

However, it is difficult to escape the conclusion that well-intentioned meddling in the industry has failed to solve any of the underlying problems. No enquiry has started from the premise that the diversity of British beers and the good features of the British pub should be protected, or even extended. No enquiry has come remotely close to analyzing how the industry can cope with over-capacity without crushing diversity underfoot.

Thousand of tenants have lost their livelihood in the name of security of tenure. The market grip of the national combines has been strengthened, in the name of weakening it. Any increased price competition will be as nothing compared with the switch to leases, with higher rents which will force up prices. Pub closures will produce the ultimate monopoly, no pub at all.

The march of competition policy has been a march of folly. The customer is still being mugged.

Stephen Cox

GLOBAL BEER

 THERE IS NOTHING new about a brewer looking to a world market in which to sell his product. As early as 1840 Scottish brewer William Younger's products were on sale in the United States and even in Rio de Janeiro. A few European contemporaries, such as Heineken and Carlsberg, had also begun to extend the scope of their markets beyond their national borders. However, it has only been in the last thirty years that we have seen the move by the world's largest brewers to create a truly global market for their products. Today Heineken, the leader in worldwide promotion, has established itself in over one hundred and fifty countries.

Back in the early 1960s, the world encompassed a rich assortment of breweries, small and large, producing a wide spectrum of beers for sale either locally or nationally. Local chauvinism, or perhaps inertia, was an important part in brand loyalty. Little of the world's total production made its way abroad, although Bass and Guinness, notably, were already selling well outside their own borders. At the start of the 1970s, most of the world's breweries were still family owned or controlled. Since that time, many have opened themselves to public subscription, either to raise money for expansion, new capital equipment or diversification. This change in the brewing industry has introduced two crucial elements. The first is that, unlike traditional family owners, shareholders are not satisfied with a static performance by the brewery; they demand ever-increasing dividends and share prices, and this takes ever-increasing growth in sales. Secondly, publicly-traded breweries have become vulnerable to speculation in their shares and to takeover bids from outside sources. The precarious nature of many breweries' financial structures coupled with sagging revenues in the 1980s, a decade in which beer consumption began to level off, if not actually decline, has led to concentration of ownership in the industry.

An easy way to increase market share, and reduce competition, is to have access to or control over the production and distribution channels of rival concerns. Over the last ten years most countries have seen a period of 'rationalisation' in their brewing industries that has left fewer active breweries and has lessened consumer choice. Now, this means of bypassing market forces is being practised on a global scale. National brewers that have outgrown their domestic markets have sought new areas to exploit, and have negotiated world-wide networks for the proliferation of their global brands.

Lager is the ammunition with which the multinationals are waging their campaigns. Taking domestic consumers for granted, the major brewers around the world have focussed on Europe. With the collapse of the Berlin Wall and the shift in the political nature of Europe, the major producers are seeking to establish themselves in Eastern Europe, where western-style marketing is still a novelty.

For the moment, however, the real centre of attention for the brewers' efforts is the United Kingdom. The key factor has been the implusive shift in British consumption from ales to limp lagers. British brewers were slow to recognise this trend; most had no lagers of their own and, therefore, have entered into licensing arrangements to produce and sell lagers, ultimately weakening markets for their own ales. The enduring exception is in Scotland, as might be expected, where Tennents have been brewing lager for more than one hundred years.

What will be the global roles of the industry leaders in the 1990s? Partnership deals, licensing agreements, takeovers, mergers and other alliances will, over the next few years, convey more and more of the world beer market into fewer and fewer hands.

Of the top ten world brewers all, bar Brahma of Brazil, have an established footing outside their own domestic market. Dramatising the importance of global brands, we have had the promise, or threat, by John Elliott to 'Fosterise' the world. Foster's epitomises globalisation: its network includes agreements with Canada's largest brewer, Molson, establishing a North American base; Courage in the EC; and Asahi, which gives access to the Japanese and Far East markets.

Anheuser-Busch, the world's largest brewer, has purchased an extensive hop farm in Bavaria and, now that the Reinheitsgebot is no longer an obstacle, would like to sell beer in Germany. It is also in the process of completing a huge amusement centre in Barcelona through which Budweiser will be sold. The attempt to secure the Budweiser-Budvar name from Czechoslovakia underscores its known intention to push its brand into those areas of Europe where at present it cannot go. In contrast, Miller seems, for the moment, to be concentrating on increasing its domestic market share.

Kirin, the second leading beer brand in the world and the fifth largest brewery, is also interested in moving directly into the European and world markets. Although claiming to be interested only in licensing arrangements, such as those with Molson in Canada and San Miguel in Hong Kong, it is only a matter of time until the Kirin, originally a mythical creature from China, is hunting for takeover prey.

The brewing assets of the financially-troubled Bond/Nathan Corporation have attracted the attention of Labatt, Canada's number two brewer. Such a takeover would move the conglomerate near to the top of the list of the world's largest producers. Labatt has already established itself in the European market by buying into two breweries in Italy, a country where there is still sales growth potential.

Even Guinness has been on the acquisition trail and now controls twenty-eight per cent of the Spanish market with the acquisition of Cruz-Campo and Union Cervecera.

International brands such as Foster's, Castlemaine, Lowenbräu, Heineken, Kronenbourg, Miller and US Budweiser have all appeared in the UK, largely via licensing agreements. To date, of the top ten mega-brewers, only Foster's has taken a direct UK stake by its purchase of Courage from Hanson Trust in 1986.

However, globalisation is not only a game played by the largest brewers. Canada's number two brewer, Labatt, has entered the UK market by signing 'partnership' deals with several regional brewers and is expected to buy outright a UK brewing facility soon. Dutch number two, Grolsch, has bought Ruddles, the cask brewery in Leicestershire, from Courage, while the Danish number three brewer, the aggressive but traditional Faxe, has recently taken a majority stake in Liverpool brewers Cains.

UK brewers are also playing a role on the world stage, as Spanish purchases by Guinness have shown. Guinness also operates seven stout plants outside the UK. Watney's Red Barrel is common outside the British Isles and Bass, Allied, Whitbread, Courage and S&N have all found markets for their products in countries around the world. Regional brewers such as Bateman's, Fuller's, Youngs and Greene King have followed the lead of the national combines.

To date, with the exception of Guinness, no UK brewery has moved to acquire brewing properties or licensing agreements in other parts of the world. However, most of the nationals are now diversifying their operation. Many of the world's largest breweries have now expanded their 'leisure' enterprises such as hotel, bar and restaurant chains, gambling and betting facilities; vineyards and distilleries; sporting teams and events; and entertainment and amusement complexes (cinemas and theme parks). British brewers are in the vanguard of this movement. To be sure, these investments will all be used as vehicles to promote the products of the brewery involved, but the relative importance of brewing has greatly diminished. As we have recently seen, for Grand Met it is now of no consequence at all.

It is not only the beer brands that are becoming international. Production and supply of malted barley, the raw ingredient for beer, is now controlled by fewer and fewer companies. Over the past few years Canada Malting, by far the world's largest maltster, has been slowly building up acquisitions, including Hugh Baird in the UK, and America's Great Western Malting. It will come as no great surprise that shareholdings in Canada Maltings are dominated by Canada's two biggest brewers, Labatt and Molson.

A large portion of beers in Canada, the US and Central and South America are produced with pale malt from Canada Malting. With all these breweries using exactly the same basic ingredient, the only recipe variable lies in the quantity used. Maris Otter, once one of the most famous of malts, has now all but disappeared from the recipes of UK brewers, as have many other varieties around the world. It's like everyone using the same teabag. As such, the future for quality and variety looks bleak.

The factor most inhibiting to the general availability of good beer over the past thirty years has been the ascendancy of the marketing specialists for whom the product itself is now barely relevant, but for whom image and visibility, together with minimised production costs, are paramount. In the next two decades advertising budgets will be the most important aspect in globalisation of the brewing industry. The world media will be saturated with manipulative advertising and sponsorship campaigns for global brands that are all form and no content, much like the beers themselves.

All this makes gloomy reading for the lover of quality traditional beer. Is there any salvation for our taste buds or will we and our descendants be condemned to drinking Bud or Foster's wherever we go in the world?

Fortunately there is hope. From San Francisco to Sydney and Orkney to the Orange Free State, new breweries and brewpubs are being set up. And the few remaining independent breweries are fighting back by looking globally for their markets.

In the coming years, this movement should prosper. World-wide micro-brewery sales increased by almost seventy per cent in 1990 and projections for the next five years show a steady increase, although in lesser annual increments. Globally, however, the movement is still exceedingly small – approximately one per cent of total world sales. The majority of the world's micro-breweries are producing 'British-style' ales as an antidote to the products that are generally available. Perhaps this is not surprising in view of the number of clones of Peter Austin's Ringwood Brewery that have now found their way to virtually every part of the globe. However, such companies will only continue to survive with the commitment of those who appreciate good beer and have not been seduced by tasteless glossy advertising into drinking tasteless international brands.

What are the next thirty years likely to bring in the brewing industry? An experienced futurist would predict that it will probably resemble today's as little as that of thirty years ago does. But, if brewers proceed as they are now, through a combination of huge advertising expenditures and 'co-operative' international agreements, sanctioned at government level, the world will be dominated by a handful of major producers and products. It will, in other words, be like the soft-drink industry.

Resisting such change will take the united efforts of an international CAMRA-style movement; this has, in fact, started to form. Beer consumer groups in Belgium, the Netherlands and the UK have formed the European Beer Consumers Union to give beer drinkers a voice in Brussels. CAMRA (Canada) collaborates regularly with its UK counterpart. And in Poland, Czechoslovakia and Germany beer lovers are starting to group together to protect their traditional brews. CAMRA membership in Australia and New Zealand is also growing and becoming more active as a protest against the products of Foster's and Lion Nathan.

We cannot be complacent, for the world's mega-brewers will not wait for any international CAMRA to form. They already have their strategies for the twenty-first century mapped out. And if appreciators of quality beer are not able to erase the handwriting on the wall, by 2001 the only beers on sale in ninety-nine per cent of the pubs, bars, cafés and liquor stores of the world will be called Foster's, Bud or Heineken.

Drew Ferguson and *Iain Loe*

LAGER – THANKS FOR THE MAMMARIES

Cleavage was an essential element of lager advertising in the 1970s. All those commercials featuring three men in a pub and a barmaid with big tits would have been pointless without it. At the time lager was desperately trying to lose its girlie pop image, and to a large extent mammaries came to the rescue.

Twenty years ago lager had a major image problem: real men drank bitter, lager was for women, kids and Southern nancy boys. In some areas of the country, it was still seen as a 'pretty poofy sort of drink' until the early 1980s, according to a leading lager's marketing director. (No doubt she is referring to those hard-bitten Northerners who wear tee-shirt and jeans in arctic conditions and think that throwing up at the end of a session shows that you've had a good time.)

The image problem was largely self-created. Lager had originally been aimed at the growing numbers of women visiting pubs. It was presented as an alternative to bitter and soft drinks that was relatively low in alcohol and easy to drink. In other words it was weak, watery and bland. In 1960 it took one per cent of the British beer market, ten years later its share had risen to a respectable, but still small, seven per cent.

Then a number of factors conspired to give brewers the opportunity to position lager as a new and different drink for the younger generation. In the 1970s, cheap package holidays give many Brits their first taste of Europe – including its lager beers, a global trend towards lighter flavours emerged, and Britain's youth culture became a potent economic force. There was also increasing evidence that drinkers were getting fed up with keg bitter, not least of which was provided by CAMRA, then a fledgling consumers' association. 'Maltade', as it is known to its many detractors, helped pave the way for lager by convincing drinkers that consistency was more important than character. But, if you are looking for someone to blame for the growth of Britain's lager culture, blame Hitler.

World War two claimed the lives of many publicans and with them were lost their essential cellar skills. After the war a new generation of publicans, unaware of the complexities of real ale, which is unpalatable if it is not kept and served properly, saw thousands of drinkers desert traditional brews in favour of bottled beers. By 1960 bottled beer accounted for 34 per cent of the market. Given the choice between often undrinkable ale and consistent, if less flavoursome, bottled beer, it is not surprising that many chose the latter.

It is equally predictable that the brewers saw the popularity of bottled beer as the start of the keg beer revolution. Keg beer is exactly the same as bottled beer, it just comes out of a bigger container. It keeps for weeks, is easy to make, requires the minimum of care, and always tastes the same. It could also command a higher price than real ale, despite often being lower in gravity and therefore cheaper to make.

Brewers quickly converted enormous production facilities to keg and ploughed millions into promoting it. They tried to create national brands with heavyweight TV campaigns that reassured drinkers that consistency was what they should be looking for. Watney took consistency to ludicrous extremes with its infamous Watney's Red campaign, which included red-socked reps and vermilion pub front doors.

To their dismay brewers found that their all-singing all-dancing, bland-enough-for-everyone brands were turning drinkers off. A significant number, given voice through CAMRA, wanted old-fashioned beer and the brewers were forced to give it back to them. Brands that had been killed off in the lemming-like rush for keg production were resurrected and new ones launched. Fortunately for the brewers, real ale brands required low-key marketing support unlike their brash keg counterparts, which left them with millions to spend on advertising their new great hope. Lager had all the production and profit advantages of keg, with the added bonus that it wasn't bitter. The brewers figured that the growing number of young men then visiting pubs would adopt something that tasted different and, after all, *was* different from what their dads drank. Lager had huge potential, they reasoned, if only it could lose its limp-wristed associations.

Enter an array of ad campaigns featuring dolly birds and lots of male bonding. Marketers now blushingly describe their early attempts to put hairs on lager's chest as 'tapping into pub culture', 'creating some interesting imagery around it' and 'showing people having fun with lager as the central source of their enjoyment'. What they really mean is leg-over advertising. The central theme of most of the early ads seems to be 'drink this and get laid'.

There are only so many things that you can do with the three men in a pub format, and the brewers tried them all to tackle lager's lack of machismo. There was the one about the bloke who ordered lager and was duly sent up by his bitter-drinking mates for wanting such a girlie drink, but who turned out to be the cleverest/sexiest/coolest of them all. Then there was the one about the bloke who didn't order lager and was ridiculed by his pals for being so old-fashioned/unhip. Either way, they all ended up ordering lager from a barmaid whose pendulous breasts were precariously squeezed into a low cut top. And, thanks to lager, they all ended up great friends having a great time. In those days the ultimate challenge was to get the slogan, the packshot and the cleavage all in the end frame.

Ads designed to boost off-licence sales were just as bad. Allied produced a real gem with its "Skolar of Arithmetic" ad, in which the Skol drinker carefully divided his cans amongst his friends so that he still had enough left 'to give Samantha one'.

It all sounds rather passé in the politically correct 1990s, but back then – when gays were still called 'queers' and feminism was known as 'women's lib' – it worked. Lager's share of the beer market rocketed from seven per cent in 1970 to almost 31 per cent by 1980. Advertising helped to create the standard lager market and has remained the most important factor ever since.

Obviously it would be nonsense to suggest that standard lager's success is based solely on advertising – not even Soho's sharp-suited admen would dare make such an extravagant claim. But many believe that people drink the advertising rather than the lager, largely because there is little to choose between the various standard brands on offer. Let's face it, they all taste pretty much the same, or in marketing-speak 'most drinkers would find all the major brands to be acceptable on taste terms'. That leaves advertising to establish a point of difference.

Few regional brewers could afford mass media ad campaigns, but that didn't stop them trying to grab a share of this lucrative market. Every brewer and his auntie launched a lager brand. Many attempted to give their pallid brews credibility by using Germanic imagery, even though their lagers bore little resemblance to the real thing. British standard lager was, and still is, a bastardised version of continental Europe's fine pale beers: it is substantially weaker in both taste and alcohol. The Europeans maintain that it is impossible to achieve a full-bodied lager flavour under 1040 degrees; as they invented this style of brewing, they ought to know what they are talking about. Most standard lagers in the UK have gravities in the 1030s and are matured for far less time than the brews on which they are based.

Never an industry to let the facts inhibit the marketing, brewers chose Germanic-sounding names and decorated their fonts and cans with castles, bears and steins. Their logic was simple: people believe that Germans brew good lager, so if we pretend that our British-brewed gnats piss has German origins people will automatically assume that it too is 'good lager'.

Years later these spurious Teutonic trappings would be sent up to great affect by a Caribbean lager, which was trying to position itself as an unpretentious premium brew. Red Stripe Jamaican lager, which is brewed in Bedfordshire, characterised its weaker competitors as "fartgerburp-hagen-steiner-meister-brau-triple X" in one of a series of hilarious radio commercials.

By the mid-Seventies national brewers had established lager as a real lad's drink and, backed by big ad budgets, their brands dominated this sizeable and profitable market. Almost all of the pioneering brands had adopted the same 'Jack the Lad' advertising strategy, which meant that as well as tasting the same their ads looked the same. Given that advertising is the 'real' point of difference, the brewers realised it was time to break out of the pub.

Heineken was the first to escape the pub rut. Created in 1975, 'Refreshes the parts that other beers cannot reach' was originally considered avant garde and extremely risky. In discussion groups, which is what marketers and admen use to find out what the punters think of their work, drinkers made comments like 'it's not proper beer advertising', 'it's not very funny so they must be serious about this refreshes the parts stuff' and 'it's enough to put you off your tea' (that referred to the policemen's feet ad which gave close-up views of some particularly ugly plates).

Heineken persevered and went on to create some of the UK's funniest and most creative beer advertising. Its perseverence paid off: it has been the second biggest lager in the pub trade and the biggest seller through off licences for years. 'Refreshes the parts' spawned a new era of lager advertising: the epic had arrived and Charlton Heston would not have looked out of place in some of them. Production budgets spiralled and the other brewers raced to find slogans fit for their brands.

However, Heineken had stolen the march on its competitors by claiming swilling lager's only real benefit – refreshment – for its own. Some of its competitors spurned the new advertising trend and stuck steadfastly to their roots, notably Courage. Before it was 'Fosterised' by the Elders takeover, its biggest lager brand was Hofmeister. The brand's spokesman for almost ten years was George, a six-foot-plus lager lout in teddy bear's clothing who was as far distanced from his Germanic relatives as the stuff that he promoted. One of lager advertising's best-loved characters, his roguish antics made Hofmeister one of the UK's biggest selling lagers. But George the Bear became a victim of his own success. His immature charm made him hugely popular with children and hugely unpopular with the Independent Broadcasting Authority, which insisted that he grow up and become less boisterous.

As the market grew and the fight for market share became more fierce, the creative challenge of lager advertising degenerated into a contest for the biggest laugh. As one adman put it: 'In the Eighties all the ads said was "this joke was brought to you by…"'

Already awash with gassy brews, Britain was then treated to the Australian lager revolution. Foster's and Castlemaine XXXX launched with huge ad spends, backed by straightforward marketing logic: Australia has a hot dusty climate and Aussies drink an awful lot of beer, therefore Brits will believe that it's good stuff. Marketers also believed that we secretly admire the tough and rugged Ocker attitude to life. Personally speaking, I have never felt the urge to commune with sheep or 'go bush'.

The social climate began to change in the Eighties, becoming less tolerant of excess and more health-conscious. The popular press vilified rampaging lager louts, and drink-driving became a major issue. Meanwhile lager drinkers were getting older, their palates had defrosted and started to mature. Premium strength lager, which is what the Continentals regarded as standard, started to take off.

The changing face of the lager market presented brewers with several challenges: to keep standard lager brands relevant and interesting to both young drinkers and their older counterparts, and to present their premium brews as different and attractive without implying that they were better than the stuff they had been pouring down people's necks for twenty years. Brewers also had to face the fact that their core consumers, 18-24 year olds, were dwindling in number and that young drinkers, brought up with slick mass media advertising, were increasingly difficult to impress. They had little choice: lager advertising had to grow up.

While some chose to stick to their advertising guns – such as Heineken, Carlsberg and Carling Black Label – and adapt long-running campaigns, others cast about for new solutions. Skol had a fling with cartoon viking Hagar the Horrible, whose favourite pastime appeared to be cudgelling his pals, and Harp tried to convince brewers that it was 'precision' brewed. Harp discovered to its cost that drinkers are not remotely interested in how standard lager is made. 'They know the difference between premium and standard lager and they don't want to be told that cooking lager is carefully crafted when they know that it's brewed in a vat the size of Stoke Poges,' comments an adman. Its late Eighties 'precision brewing' campaign did for Harp what Edwina Currie did for egg sales.

Incidentally, Tennent's Pilsner is now challenging the marketing truism that product information bores standard lager drinkers rigid. It claims that its latest campaign, which says that it is made with Czechoslovakian yeast and is 'brewed to taste a bit different', has turned the brand's fortunes around, from 'double figure volume decline' to 'double digit growth'.

Harp then flirted with Johnathan Ross, of shoulder pads, speech impediment and chat show fame, in its 'get sharp to Harp' campaign. Like George the Bear and Hagar the Horrible, Ross fell foul of the IBA's code of conduct, which was tightened in 1988, because he was deemed to have too much kid appeal.

By the late Eighties standard lager had reached its peak and premium lagers were gaining ground on that once invincible market. Changing consumer attitudes, increasing competition and slowly declining volumes forced brewers to take their humour more seriously.

Eventually the joke-sponsored 1980s gave way to the wry, more cerebral 1990s – except for Castlemaine, which preferred the idea that Australians wouldn't give a f*** for new manism – and a new advertising trend of unpretentiousness was born. Cynics say the trend started because brewers recognised that they didn't have a lot to be pretentious about. Heineken decided to position itself as the Robin Hood of the lager world (honestly, that is what its marketing director and ad agency said), based on the idea that 'when something isn't right Heineken puts it right'. Foster's tried to become the trade mark of a laid-back lifestyle, drunk by people with confidence, insight and a wry sense of humour, while Harp clasped unpretentiousness to its liquid bosom. Meanwhile Skol and Hofmeister, deprived of TV exposure, lost volume and became price-fighting brands.

The less said about Heineken's Locksleyesque ambitions the better. At the time, Foster's had to do something. Paul Hogan established it as the no worries 'amber nectar' in the mid-Eighties, but by the end of the decade he had moved to more lucrative movie pastures and had become a tad too wrinkled to communicate with Britain's media-literate youth. His successor, Burt Lancaster, didn't last long. If Hogan was getting a bit pruney, Lancaster was positively crevassed, but he had a different role to play. Lancaster starred in the 'pass it on' campaign, which was supposed to communicate a 'no worries' attitude to life in a more mature way. In the first ad, he met a young huckster who taught him to lie back, relax and renounce his cares. In the second, he 'passed it on' to an overworked thirty-something executive by playing a video game named space monkeys (seriously). It is rumoured that there was to be a third ad in which the aforementioned exec 'passes it on' to a colleague, but the campaign was canned before it could get that far.

Foster's new solution was to create a campaign featuring ordinary-looking blokes who could smile at life's misfortunes. 'Don't you just hate it when that happens?' asks the camera. 'Foster's. Don't you just love it?' asks the pseudo-Aussie voice-over. Catchy eh? Foster's hopes that the above will become a new national catchphrase.

Harp is trying to dress up old gags in new livery and claim them for its own in its 'time for a sharp exit' campaign. In marketing speak that equates to 'using extreme representations of life's awkward moments'. In 1991 that meant variations on 'whoops I've forgotten my trousers' and the scissor-happy hairdresser joke. If Harp, Foster's and Heineken indicate the shape of lager marketing to come, brewers run the severe risk of disappearing up their own lauter tuns. No doubt when Nineties caring and sharing has lost its vogue, they will invent a new advertising bandwagon to jump on. Perhaps we will see a right bastard backlash and a return to get-it-down-your-neck advertising. Perhaps not. Meanwhile the brewers can reflect on their creative achievements.

After all, lager advertising has come a long way from its breast-dependent days. Lines like 'Australians wouldn't give a XXXX for anything else' and 'is simeone pulling your pilsner' are, of course, far more subtle and witty than the vulgar ones used to convince young men in days of yore that lager wasn't girlie pop. Aren't they?

Ruth Nicholas

THE GBG – THE BEER LOVERS' BIBLE

The *Good Beer Guide* is, and always has been, a true labour of love. Each year, CAMRA members all over Britain are galvanised into action, to engage in their favourite pursuit in the interests of research, enlightenment and the common good. Every February they are urged to visit as many pubs as they can, inspection forms in hand, to seek out the best beer in the land. Not an onerous task, one might think, indeed in many respects a very pleasurable one, but considering the Guide now carries some five thousand pubs, it is a job that has to be done properly (GBG editors are very demanding!). Without the unpaid efforts of these volunteers, the Guide simply would not exist.

In essence, the Guide has not changed in all its years of publication. It was the first and only guide to concentrate on the pleasures of beer drinking. Other guides may lead the consumer to pretty country pubs with continental cuisine – so does the GBG – but first and foremost it is a guide for beer lovers. To this end, it is more than just a guide, but also a campaigning tool, which does not shirk controversy and has had some notable successes.

The early guides concentrated almost entirely on spreading the word about real ale, educating its readers in what it is and why they should eschew the fizzy keg stuff that was all that was on offer in most pubs when the Guide first came out in 1974. As the readership demanded more sophistication, other issues became predominant, such as the big brewers' dedication to ripping the heart out of the village local to replace it with a 'theme' pub; Neil Hanson's controversial 'heavy metals' article that accused brewers of an increasing use of unwanted additives that can give unpleasant side-effects; the recently-won battle for changes in the licensing hours; and the implications of the M&MC Report.

CAMRA lawyers are often required to scour the text with a fine toothed comb to make sure the editors do not go too far, as was the case with the very first Guide (ed. John Hanscomb) which had to be reprinted to withdraw the statement that Watney's beers should be avoided 'like the plague'. 'Plague' copies of the Guide are now, incidentally, collectors' items. CAMRA itself paid £100 for a copy in 1988.

The Guide has seen several editors (some having stayed the course longer than others), and has grown enormously since the four founder CAMRA members first had the idea of producing a list of recommended ale-houses.

The prototype for the Guide was researched by eager members of the fledgling campaign; it was a typewritten, duplicated affair, put together on a table in Michael Hardman's front room. Only a couple of hundred copies were produced. The first, pukka published edition (cover price 75p) appeared a year later, in 1974, compiled – again on a voluntary basis – by John Hanscomb and his deputy, Tim Linfoot. In those early days, CAMRA members were still very thin on the ground in some parts of the country. Indeed, Scotland did not appear in the guide at all until 1975 (and even today it is hard to cover pubs in outlying areas). For the first edition,

John Hanscomb researched a whole county single-handedly in one day – and this was before all-day opening came into force.

The first Guide listed 1500 pubs with simple one-sentence descriptions. It is a sign of the development of real ale that this edition did not list beers by name, but just gave the brewer and type of beer available at each pub, ie bitter, mild or strong ale. It wasn't until 1977 that a brewery's different beers were distinguished by reference number, then in 1979 all the beers were listed by name for each pub as they are today.

The brewery section in the first Guide made very brief and rather unhappy reading. A few sample entries read as follows:

Barnsley: *A shadow of its former self; due to close*
Gibbs Mew: *A disaster*
Holden: *Too much gassy beer*
Harvey: *Difficult to find real ale*

Contrasting with this though were the promising:

Jennings: *Real beer is the rule*
Bateman: *Generally excellent*
Theakston: *Highly recommended*

The London brewer, Fuller, Smith and Turner, was listed as having only a handful of draught houses, which is indicative of the successful campaigning of the Guide and CAMRA members in general: they now supply real ale to all but three of their 200 tied houses. The importance of the brewery section and its possible effectiveness was already recognised by the second edition of the Guide (ed. Michael Hardman), when it covered six pages. The number of brew-pubs was slowly growing: it had increased from just four to six. The brewery section has gone on from strength to strength, and took up some 83 pages of the last edition. The latest significant development was the introduction of tasting notes in 1989 (ed. Andrea Gillies) in an attempt to give beers the same respect as wines.

By second edition, the Guide really began to find its feet, and was set to establish itself as a bestseller. The Campaign was now in a position to pay a full-time editor of publications (Michael Hardman), and under his leadership, the Guide took on a new (and unusual) format which still makes it readily noticed on the bookshop shelves today.

Each editor has brought to the Guide his or her own particular style within the strictures of the established format and presentation. Different typefaces and page designs have been tried over the years, with every editor determined to have a go at something new. While the Guide has been printed in black only since 1984, it had used two colours from 1976, with the occasional splash of full colour during Roger Protz's editorship. Another variation is the use of the maps, which have been tried all together at the back of the book and, as now, at the start of each chapter. Each method has its advantages and disadvantages.

Where the individual editors have the most scope is in their choice of cover. To create a cover that is appealing, campaigning, and which will please the editor *and* the National Executive is probably the most difficult and angst-making part of the whole project. Design submissions are pored over, rejected and reconsidered, in varying states of intoxification, many times before a decision is taken, and very rarely does the resulting work of art please everyone. There have been exceptions: the 1992 guide (ed. Jeff Evans) was greeted with general approval and enthusiasm. The consensus at CAMRA HQ that year was that he'd got it right, and that's a tough test to pass.

The other place for individual editors to make their mark is naturally in the editorial section. Here he or she has the opportunity to get over important current campaigning issues, but also any particular subject dear to their own hearts. This was a gift for the Guide's only woman editor to date, Andrea Gillies, who took the opportunity to invite not one but *three* women journalists to write articles for the 1989 edition.

Andrea's appointment as editor of this bastion of maleness was greeted, not unexpectedly, with some furore (and in some cases incredulity) by stolid (male) CAMRA members and the press. For the Campaign of course, the media interest was a real boon: at a time when coverage of CAMRA was at a fairly low ebb, here was something journalists could get their teeth into. Immediately on her appointment, Andrea was caught up in a whirlwind of some forty press, radio and TV interviews. Never before or since has she posed with so many pints of beer in an effort to prove that women do drink the stuff, and what's more actually like it.

Over the years, the Guide has contributed substantially to the Campaign's funds, selling consistently well to members and the general public. It peaked in 1979, when CAMRA was persuaded by the new distributors, Arrow, to print 90,000 copies in their determination to make it the biggest-selling beer book ever. It did achieve a massive 70,000 sale, but CAMRA was left to pick up the tab for the 20,000 that remained unsold. The print run has been rather more conservative in recent years, but has been steadily rising again since 1989. The 1992 45,000 print run was boosted by a reprint of a further 5,000 copies.

Since 1988, some of the production costs have been met by the generous sponsorship of British Coal (then the Solid Fuel Advisory Service), who also took over most of the responsibility for organising the book's annual launch party.

These days, in the face of stiffer competition (bookshop shelves are full of pub and leisure guides), the *Good Beer Guide* is still the only one to concentrate on the real issues of importance to the lover of real ale and real pubs. There is always something new to campaign for, even though the battle for the production of real ale has been won. The *Good Beer Guide* is read by the brewers, and through its pages we must continue to press them to cater for our readership, and not the demands of their accountants. Our readers want more guest beers, improved facilities at pubs, including no-smoking areas, better amenities for the disabled, children's certificates and so on. The *GBG* will go on demanding them for many years to come.

GOOD BEER GUIDE EDITORS

1974 *John Hanscomb*	1978-83 *Roger Protz*	1989-90 *Andrea Gillies*
1975-77 *Michael Hardman*	1984-88 *Neil Hanson*	1991- *Jeff Evans*

Jill Adam

THE MYSTERIES OF THE ORGANISATION

Introduction

Like all organisations, CAMRA has both formal and informal structures, and a distinctive organisational culture not entirely unrelated to its subject-matter and habitat (beer and pubs).

This article necessarily presents an insider's view of CAMRA, counterbalanced elsewhere in this book by views from outsiders. Nonetheless, it attempts to be analytic, and is certainly the product of long observation of the organisation at work.

Though CAMRA is (in principle and in practice) an egalitarian organisation, in the sense of being non-racist, non-sexist, non-ageist and so on, the distribution of the membership has influenced the nature of the movement. Over 40% of members live in London, the South-East and East Anglia, mirroring the distribution of the UK population. In the North, Yorkshire is numerically the strongest region, while Scotland and Wales (especially North Wales) manifest much lower interest in membership. CAMRA has always, therefore, been basically English, to the extent that compensating factors have had to be built in almost by design (eg in the extra-constitutional tradition that there is a member from Scotland on the National Executive).

In profile, the "average CAMRA member" is a white early-middle-aged middle-class Southern English male in a professional or middle managerial occupation. There are marked regional differences, and any attender of CAMRA events may well find that most activists do not match the profile, but (considered demographically) the people who customarily become Branch committee members, Regional Directors and National Executive members are broadly representative of their electorate in the membership of the Campaign. The periodic internal attacks on CAMRA's leadership and perspective for being "too southern oriented" are indicative of a general perception of the effects of population and membership distribution by region, which translates roughly in electoral terms into the distribution of NE members.

In common with trends elsewhere in business and public life, the number of women in the Campaign, and their level of activism, has risen steadily over its 21 years of existence. A key factor in this is that since 1970, it has become more common for women to use pubs and drink beer, and in a symbiotic development, the pub environment and male behaviour have become more hospitable and receptive to, and even encouraging of, this trend. As far as the Campaign's public image is concerned, however, perception lags behind reality, so that whenever a woman takes a high-profile position in CAMRA (Margaret Clark-Monks becoming the first female member of the NE in the mid-1970s, Andrea Gillies the first female Editor of the *Good Beer Guide* appointed in 1988, and Christine Cryne the first female Organiser of the Great British Beer Festival in 1992) the media response is astonished curiosity tinged with semi-humorous disbelief.

The operation of the Campaign is distinguished by its conviviality and good fellowship. There are two main reasons for this. First, CAMRA has taken on something of the character of the industry which is its chief concern. Brewing, especially up to and through the 1970s, had an atmosphere of a craft guild, with mutual help common even between "competitors". Though this characteristic is slowly being bled out of the industry under recessionary pressures and the predominance of accountants and marketing men over brewers, it still survives in many of the medium-sized independent brewers, such as Adnams, Morlands, Hall and Woodhouse, Bateman's, Fuller's and Timothy Taylors. The pervasive power of this "craft ideal", combining professional pride, a close-knit family feeling, and what can only be called the romance of brewing, can be judged by the number of CAMRA members who have been involved in setting up new small breweries.

Second, virtually every CAMRA meeting takes place in a pub or club – with the notable exception of the National Finance and General Purposes Committee, which meets at HQ. Meetings of Finance and the National Executive are "dry" (alcohol is not consumed during the meeting), but even they adjourn to the bar at the close of business. This means that the formal and informal modes of operation are never far apart, and even the most serious and complex business has a social side. A point missed in the formal meeting can be made almost immediately afterwards informally, and a difference of opinion can have its hard edges softened by a further discussion over a pint or two. So many good ideas and plans come out of the post-meeting chat that it can be difficult to convince doubters that real business does get done in the meeting as well, and that CAMRA is not just "the society for good excuses for going to the pub". (Not, of course, that one should ever need an excuse for going to the pub!)

The final major factors which shape the culture of CAMRA are individualism and voluntaryism. Joining CAMRA is a conservative form of protest about unwelcome changes in beers, breweries and pubs, or a more radical protest about the structure of the brewing industry. The individuals attracted to join CAMRA tend to be those who by their nature do not accept others' decisions without question or challenge, who are of decided views and not afraid to air them publicly and to follow them through into demonstrative action. Leadership of the movement is thus an exercise in political tactics well expressed in the phrase "like trying to herd cats", for unity cannot be achieved in all circumstances by appeals to the movement's larger aims and passionate communication of a wider vision. At the expense of inconsistency to outside observers, on some issues a measure of "freedom of conscience" has to be allowed if firmly-held minority views cannot be accommodated in a consensus.

This catholicity is emphasised by movement's voluntaryism. One cannot order CAMRA members to do anything. They are all volunteers. They have to want to do something, and have to be motivated to do it. Leadership has to be by equally voluntary example. Though harmless forms of self-promotion can play a part (such as putting a view with passion and articulacy in a speech to the AGM, or writing an article in *What's Brewing*), office in the Campaign is more often achieved by the sheer weight of one's voluntary effort and input (for instance in running a local Branch or working at the Great British Beer Festival) which can be judged and appreciated by fellow members.

Finally, there are of course different views in CAMRA itself of the type of organisation it is, or should be. Some members think of it as a trade union, which should have mandated delegates and branch block votes. Some see it as an antiquarian society, preserving all that is best of the past in terms of brewery buildings, pubs, the paraphernalia of beer, and the ales themselves. Some want it to be a radical protest group, taking direct action and adopting confrontational tactics. Others see it simply as a local or widely dispersed drinking club, a social network of friends. Yet others take a primarily managerial interest in running it as a business, or in manipulating its politics, or in publishing books about beer. While all of these have an element of truth, they are all partial: none gives the full picture. CAMRA is itself alone, and has a uniqueness deriving from its history, culture, aims, subject-matter, achievements, and the people involved.

The following sections pick out some key points on CAMRA's structure and operation.

Constitution

CAMRA's written constitution is its Memorandum and Articles of Association, adopted when it became a company limited by guarantee in 1976. The Memorandum sets out the organisation's broad aims as follows:

(a) To take over the assets and liabilities of the Campaign for Real Ale and to enter into such Agreements and to take all such steps as may be necessary for that purpose.

(b) To protect the interests of all those who wish to drink real beer.

(c) To campaign for an improvement in the quality and variety of British beer.

(d) To draw to the attention of members and the general public those places where real beer can be found.

(e) To promote and foster activities concerned with the consumption of good quality beer.

(f) To campaign for the retention and reinstatement of the facilities of the traditional British pub including the public bar.

(g) To ensure in every manner possible that producers and retailers of beer act in the best interests of the customer.

(h) To ensure that the knowledge and expertise of brewing real beer is kept alive.

(i) To improve the standards of food, drink (whether intoxicating or not), service, hygiene and facilities in all establishments subject to the provisions of the Licensing Act 1964 or any subsequent similar legislation.

(j) To publish and issue to members magazines or news letters.

(k) To publish or sponsor the publication of books, articles, magazines, photographs, films, radio and television programmes or any similar material connected in any way with the items mentioned above, and to market them and otherwise assist in the collection and dissemination of information.

A number of significant points arise from the Memorandum and Articles. First, the building-block of the Campaign is the individual member. Branches have no constitutional status, and no locus in proceedings at the AGM. At meetings, the "one member, one vote" principle applies universally. Second, the only body or committee created (apart from the AGM) is the National Executive, of up to 12 members, who serve for a term of up to 3 years and are eligible for re-election. The NE has full directorial powers between AGMs (though the possibility exists of an extra-ordinary general meeting requisitioned by members). All other national committees, and Branches and the areas they cover, depend on the constitutional powers granted to the NE.

Third, CAMRA is specifically established as a non-political organisation, in the sense of not being aligned with any political party. Obviously, much that CAMRA does is "political", in that it involves issues of public policy, whether that is on fiscal matters such as excise duty rates, on health matters such as alcohol consumption, or on public order matters such as the link between pub design and violence. But several moves to identify CAMRA politically as supporting any party have been soundly defeated whenever proposed at AGMs.

The AGM

The CAMRA National Conference and AGM has three roles:
- to conduct the statutory business required at the annual general meeting of a limited company, such as receiving the report of the directors (the NE), approving and adopting the annual accounts, appointing the auditors, and appointing the directors
- to establish policy by debate on motions submitted
- to inform and inspire further campaigning.

The first of these roles is usually fulfilled speedily and efficiently, though full opportunity is given for questioning of the NE members chairing the four key committees (Finance and General Purposes, Strategy and Promotions, Branches, and Economics Industry and Government).

The second is more problematic. The average member who attends the National Conference and AGM enjoys the theatricality and knockabout fun of adversarial debate, and probably feels passionately about several of the 40 or so motions for debate usually submitted. But viewed diachronically, as I found in the early 1980s when I codified AGM decisions in the first Policy File, the CAMRA AGM spends a good deal of time debating the same topics year after year. Attempts to restrict the submission of motions (for instance, by requiring 5 or more sponsors or submission from a quorate Branch meeting) have been unsuccessful, and it is still the case that any two CAMRA members can submit a motion. Theoretically, the AGM/Standing Orders Sub-Committee has power to composite motions which duplicate each other, but proposers often resist even this. The only way of ensuring that important new policy areas are given adequate discussion is by the classification of motions into 4 categories: motions which involve new policy, or major amendments to existing policy, relating to external affairs; motions which involve internal administrative matters, or alter existing policy only marginally; motions within broad existing policy which are either already being actioned, or will be if no dissent is expressed; and motions which are already policy which the proposers nonetheless refuse to withdraw. Debate is focussed on the first two categories.

The key problem is that in policy terms, CAMRA is a mature organisation. There are few major new developments each year which warrant some 600 members sitting for half-an-hour or more in semi-solemn council to resolve and vote upon. Yet each year, around 40 motions of varying relevance are submitted.

As with all mass audiences, the AGM is susceptible to oratory based on unashamed and passionate appeals to basic principles. But it is rare, however passionate the debate, for commonsense to be entirely lacking from decisions. Over the years, the AGM has shown itself to be a good judge of a case and a character.

The third role is one which has been developed over the 1980s, by devices such as inviting prominent speakers or organising workshop sessions on practical issues – anything to avoid the waste of time of having several hundred people sitting around while debate takes place on a motion calling for a symbol to be introduced in the *Good Beer Guide* to indicate pubs where darts are played. Finally, the National Conference and AGM, like all conferences, has a social side. There is invariably an accompanying beer festival, usually visits to local breweries, and generally all the other activities well-known to conference goers...

The National Executive, its Committees and Officers
The National Executive has changed markedly in its mode of operation since the early days of CAMRA. First, it is more stable group now, in the sense that turnover of NE members in the first five years of the Campaign was high, and it was rare in the 1970s for the Chairman to serve for two years or more. Through the 1980s and currently, it has become usual for NE members to serve for at least two terms of office (six years), and for the Chairman to serve for two to three years. The continuity of control has been helpful as the issues faced have become more complex and long-term in their solutions. The drawback is that talented "new blood" is perhaps deterred by the difficulty of securing electon to the NE. It is rare for an NE member who stands for re-election to be defeated. Second, the NE's process has changed from the operational to the strategic, as more business has been delegated to sub-committees co-ordinated by the four key committees. This has freed the NE from the need to consider and decide upon matters of detail, such as the beer order for the Great British Beer Festival, the features schedule for *What's Brewing*, or what type of promotional pens to order, and to concentrate on policy issues.

Third, the NE's process of decision-making is less polarised and adversarial than it was in the 1970s and early 1980s. Early sessions of the NE were marked by set-piece clashes over policy issues, exacerbated occasionally by personal animosities, and sometimes resulting in the precipitate resignation of an NE member who could not abide by "cabinet responsibility" once a vote had been taken. Even in the early 1980s, one such resignation occurred ostensibly on the weighty matter of entry charges for the GBBF. Now that CAMRA is "mature" in policy terms, the NE is not so often debating those fundamental principles which give opportunity for profound and irreconcilable differences of opinion, so major disagreements are relatively rare. The NE has since the mid-1980s been a fairly homogeneous group with a common approach, and it may be that more dissent and constructive questioning of decisions would be valuable to allow alternative views to be put.

The NE meets approximately every 8 weeks, and entrusts implementation of decisions to a network of committees, which it creates each year after the National Conference and AGM, and to the Campaign's staff. There are four main committees: first, Financial and General Purposes, which comments on all activities which have a financial aspect and also oversees the operation of HQ. It is not immodest to say that since the early 1980s, with a combination of a series of strong chairmen, a highly professional membership, and greatly improved systems at HQ under the leadership of Iain Dobson, Finance Committee has guided CAMRA to results which would be the envy of a great number of small companies and membership organisations.

Second, Strategy and Promotions Group, created in the mid-1980s, functions both as an internal think-tank analysing and updating CAMRA's strategy, and as a co-ordinating group directing all aspects of the Campaign's external promotion, informed whenever possible by our own market research carried out by a specialist sub-group.

Third, the Economics Industry and Government Group, formed in the early 1980s, analyses developments in the brewing industry and pub trade and directs campaigning at European, national and local levels on complex and often long-term issues, such as monopolies, prices, ingredients labelling, a sliding scale of excise duty, and so on.

Fourth and finally, Branches Committee aims to co-ordinate the activity of Branches, for instance in surveying pubs, and to draw in and interpret intelligence from the local level so that industry plans and developments can be deduced and countered even before they are explicit.

These four main groups each have specialist sub-groups, which deal for instance with investments, the use of computers in HQ and Branches, technical brewing matters, publications, and membership promotion.

In addition to appointing all national committee members, the NE also appoints its own Chairman (usually year by year, at its first meeting after the National Conference and AGM) and a number of other national officers for specific functions, such as the Staff Liaison Director, the "Scrutineers" who attempt to ensure that Branch beer festival proposals are organisationally and financially sound, and the co-ordinators for brewery liaison. Every brewery and major pub chain has a CAMRA liaison officer, whose job it is to keep track of developments, put CAMRA views over to the brewery, and feed back information to CAMRA Branches and national committees through regular reports. This system is intended to ensure that CAMRA gets up-to-date information on what is going on "on the ground" all over the UK. Though achievement is never 100% (some Branches forget to give information to brewery liaison officers, and some BLOs "go native" and end up being more on the side of the brewery than of CAMRA), the system does produce a large amount of intelligence about commercial plans.

Regions and branches

Between the national policy-making bodies and the operational bar-front face of CAMRA are the Regional Directors. They are vital communication and co-ordination links, providing intelligence from their areas to the central organisation and also providing local and regional leadership. Charged with co-ordinating Branch efforts and input (from collating entries for the *Good Beer Guide* through to deciding regional approaches to brewery policy), they are probably the hardest-worked and least-appreciated level of the Campaign's organisation.

The Campaign's 170 Branches are highly diverse in size, activity, focus and interests. Some, such as Norwich, Derby and Cambridge, have for years run major beer festivals, have produced a regular local newsletter of high quality distributed free through pubs, have produced guides to real ale pubs locally, and have been generally active in all forms of campaigning activity. Others, with few members, a wide geographical area (such as mid-Wales or the west of Scotland) to cover, and sometimes (as in Devon) a huge number of pubs, have found it difficult to muster enough people to carry out the basic annual tasks such as surveying for the *Good Beer Guide*. All have a committee to run the Branch affairs, a defined geographical area agreed with their Regional Director, and usually a programme of social events (ranging from brewery trips to fielding a team in the pub quiz league) which aims to attract new members and refresh older ones.

Though members are allocated to a Branch on the basis of where they live, they do not have to attend Branch meetings or help in any way with local campaigning. The Branch is really a voluntary association of the active members in the area. As such, what it does is dependent entirely on the individual and collective capacity and will of the members who attend meetings and do the work. The strength of the Branch system is two-fold: first, it provides some immediate and tangible activity through which local members can contribute directly to the Campaign; and second, it means that whatever the Campaign says or does is usually replicated 170 times at the local level. For instance, if a national CAMRA news release criticises beer price rises, on the basis of survey information collected by local Branches, the local media inevitably turn to the Chairman or press officer of the local CAMRA Branch to give the local angle on the story. In this way, CAMRA's impact is multiplied many times. In addition, the Branch network is the training and proving ground for virtually all those members who lead the Campaign nationally. An understanding and appreciation of how things work at the grass-roots is essential in a voluntary organisation.

Headquarters

CAMRA has never had more than 10 full-time permanent paid staff at its HQ in St. Albans. (The Editors of *What's Brewing* and the *Good Beer Guide*, and the Deputy Editor of the latter, are part-time contract appointments.)

Under Chief Executive Iain Dobson, who deals with major financial and policy issues, the staff handle membership, financial and sales administration, co-ordinate and carry out campaigning and research, produce *What's Brewing* and other publications, create national publicity, answer a non-stop flow of enquiries from all over the world, and advise and service all the national committees.

CAMRA's income derives principally from membership subscriptions, sales of books and products, the national Great British Beer Festival, donations from Branches and individuals, and miscellaneous sources such as advertising revenue from *What's Brewing* and investment interests and dividends. (A portfolio of brewery shares is maintained to give access to company annual reports and AGMs.) Expenditure falls into three main categories: the HQ costs (staff salaries, premises costs, and general office running costs), the costs of producing *What's Brewing* and mailing it to each member once a month, and general campaigning costs including expenditure on running the national committees and the regional network. No sponsorship or donation which would compromise CAMRA's independence is accepted, nor is expenditure sanctioned which would directly support one individual brewery rather than another, except in the cases of takeover targets. Even then, CAMRA has been remarkably even-handed, supporting predators when they have become victims of larger predators: the principle is that more independent breweries are a good thing for consumer choice.

Conclusion
CAMRA's organisation has evolved intelligently and gradually over the 21 years of its existence, adapting itself to new circumstances and new tasks. Since the 1980s, there has been a new effort to forecast the future and plan a medium-term campaigning and organisational strategy to meet it.

But ultimately, CAMRA as a voluntary organisation can only be directed and managed up to a point. The national leadership can point the way, but to achieve its ends, it must carry the majority of members with it. In performing this delicate political balancing act, it helps immeasurably that there is no dividing line between the local Branch level and the national level, since virtually all national committee members are or have been leaders of their Branches, and all are equally volunteers with a common campaigning aim – to preserve, promote and enjoy good beer.

Tony Millns

POSTSCRIPT: THE FUTURE

 A T THE BEGINNING of the 1980s, it would have been difficult to predict that CAMRA would enter the following decade in a state of such health. Membership at 32,000 and rising. Owners of our own (fully paid for) office accommodation. An influential, if not necessarily always agreed with, voice in the brewing industry.

Accordingly, to conclude this essentially retrospective book, with a synopsis of how the Campaign might develop in the 1990s, is a daunting prospect.

There are, however, clues for what is to come in what is happening today:

– the acquisition of Cain's brewery in Liverpool by Faxe of Denmark;
– Ruddle's, once a proud international real ale brewer, going Dutch through ownership by Grolsch;
– and, perhaps most ominous of all, the proposed merger of the brewing interests of Carlsberg and Allied Breweries.

The initial foray by foreign brewing interests into the UK beerage did not result in any immediate pursuers. Courage, for a while a reluctant member of the Hanson conglomerate, was sold off for marriage to Aussie mega-brewer Fosters, itself a product of merger mania down under.

Despite its parent giving the appearance of being in severe financial straits, Courage subsequently acquired the brewing interests of Grand Metropolitan. With a whimper, not a bang, the harbinger of the keg revolution, the ever so infamous bringer of Grotneys Red, quietly slipped off the brewing stage.

The fall-out from that "merger" has already led to the re-birth of Ushers of Trowbridge as an independent, regional brewer, and to Tony Ruddle being employed by his third "parent" since selling his family firm into the clutches of what was then one of the Big 6.

The lessons to be drawn from these seemingly endless games of pass-the-parcel had been learnt some time previously. Globalisation of world markets, and more particularly the full removal of trade barriers within the European Community, means that the UK brewing industry is no longer the cosy property of the old-style beerage.

The consumer cannot stand idly by. The threat to traditional brewing is the same whether you are in the UK or in Belgium, Holland or Germany. To combat this threat, consumers are getting together. CAMRA has joined with its sister organisations in Holland (PINT) and in Belgium (OBP) to form the European Beer Consumers Union (EBCU). We are now looking out for similar groups across Europe to join us in the campaign to protect good beer from the worst excesses of some of those who manufacture it.

While CAMRA will continue to campaign vigorously on the domestic front, it will increasingly be required to act in a concerted way with its European partners. It will be this dimension which will, more and more, influence the way in which the Campaign develops.

Consumer organisations will never be able to counter the financial resources of the multi-national brewers. However, careful husbanding and focussing of their resources will be used to continue to educate the drinker about the different beer styles not only across the length and breadth of Europe, but around the whole world.

It is important for the consumer to know the difference between Budweiser from Budvar in Czechoslavakia and the less than exciting beer of the same name from the USA. It will be no help if British drinkers are fully aware of the differences between cask beer and keg if they do not know the difference between a lambic and a gueuze.

It is far from satisfactory for the consumer if brewers push brands, ill-regarded in their domestic markets, onto an overseas drinker, gullible through lack of knowledge. If the style of brewing a classic beer such as Pilsner Urquell should change, then the consumer, whether in Manchester or Malmö, needs to know.

It will be CAMRA's responsibility to ensure that the consumer does know. That will be the challenge for the 1990s, a challenge which can be faced with confidence and a certainty that ultimately the drinker wants a quality beer, not an ersatz apology pandering to the taste of the lowest common denominator.

John M Cryne

NOTES ON CONTRIBUTORS

JILL ADAM has been Deputy Editor of the *Good Beer Guide* since 1987, and is Editor of CAMRA's guidebook *Pubs for Families*.

TIM AMSDEN was Chairman of CAMRA from 1980 to 1982.

GEORGE BATEMAN is Chairman of George Bateman and Son Ltd. of Wainfleet, Lincolnshire.

JOHN BISHOPP, a research chemist, was a member of CAMRA's National Executive in the mid-1970s.

CHRIS BRUTON was Chairman of CAMRA from 1976 to 1978.

STEPHEN COX is CAMRA's Campaigns and Communications Manager.

JOHN CRYNE is the current Chairman of CAMRA.

DREW FERGUSON is the President of CAMRA Canada.

ANTHONY FULLER is Chairman of Fuller, Smith and Turner plc of Chiswick, and a former Chairman of the Brewers' Society.

BRIAN GLOVER, a journalist, was Editor of *What's Brewing* from 1978 to 1988 and wrote *The New Beer Guide*, a book on the small brewery revolution.

MICHAEL HARDMAN is one of the four founders of CAMRA and was its first Chairman.

RICHARD HARVEY was in charge of public relations for the launch of Draught Burton Ale by Allied Breweries in 1976, and is now a freelance PR consultant.

IAN HORNSEY, formerly an academic microbiologist, is now head brewer at Nethergate Brewery.

CHRISTOPHER HUTT was the second Chairman of CAMRA, author of *The Death of the English Pub*, became Managing Director of CAMRA (Real Ale) Investments Ltd., and now runs a chain of free houses.

MICHAEL JACKSON, author of *The World Guide to Beer* and presenter of *The Beer Hunter* on Channel 4 TV, is the world's leading beer writer.

IAIN LOE is CAMRA's Research Manager and contributes a "city news" column to *What's Brewing*.

ALLAN McLEAN has been the beer columnist of *The Scotsman* since 1988, and has twice won the British Guild of Beer Writers Gold Tankard award.

TONY MILLNS was Chairman of CAMRA from 1982 to 1985.

RUTH NICHOLAS is a journalist on *Marketing Week*.

SUSAN NOWAK is a freelance journalist and Editor of CAMRA's *Guide to Good Pub Food*.

ROGER PROTZ is Editor of *What's Brewing*, edited the *Good Beer Guide* from 1978 to 1983, has written several books on beer and brewing, and contributes regular pieces on beer to newspapers, radio and TV.

JIM SCANLON was Chairman of CAMRA from 1985 to 1987.

MARTIN SYKES was a member of CAMRA's National Executive in the early 1970s, and started the first small brewery after the foundation of CAMRA.

BILL TIDY, the well-known cartoonist, contributes a regular cartoon strip (Kegbuster) to *What's Brewing*.

RICHARD WILSON is Senior Lecturer in the School of Social and Economic Studies, University of East Anglia, and the author of *Greene King: A Business and Family History*.

JOHN YOUNG is Chairman of Young & Co. of Wandsworth.

SO WHY NOT JOIN CAMRA?

IF YOU'VE READ AND ENJOYED this book – and you're not yet a CAMRA member – why not join us in the fight for good beer and pubs?

Membership brings you a copy of *What's Brewing*, the only independent monthly journal which carries news and views on what is happening in the brewing industry in the UK and worldwide.

It also entitles you to substantial discounts off various CAMRA books and products – the best-selling *Good Beer Guide* for instance is usually at least £2 cheaper for members – and reduced or free entrance to most beer festivals.

Plus there is the knowledge that in joining, you are contributing to CAMRA's efforts to fight for good beers, traditional breweries, and local pubs, for everyone who enjoys them.

If you leave it to others, you may wake up one day soon to find *your* local pub shut, *your* local brewery closed down or taken over, and *your* favourite beer no longer being brewed.

Can you afford *not* to join? Sign the form below and send it off today!

(A full list of CAMRA books and products will be sent to you with your membership package, together with details of any current special introductory offers for new members).

APPLICATION FOR CAMRA MEMBERSHIP

I/We wish to join the Campaign for Real Ale Limited, and agree to abide by the Memorandum and Articles of Association of the Campaign.

NAME(S) .... DATE ....

ADDRESS ....

....

.... POSTCODE ....

SIGNATURE ....

TELEPHONE NUMBER(S) ....

I/We enclose remittance for individual/joint membership for one year.

U.K.	£10	☐	**Joint membership**	£12	☐
Overseas	£14	☐	**Joint membership**	£16	☐
Students/Retired/Unemployed/					
Disabled	£5	☐	**Joint membership**	£6	☐

Please send your remittance (payable to CAMRA Limited) with this application form to:-
THE MEMBERSHIP SECRETARY, CAMRA LTD., 34 ALMA ROAD, ST. ALBANS, HERTS AL1 3BW